A Cornish Rhapsody

A Cornish Rhapsody

From a Penny Halfpenny an hour to a Fortune

Rudi Mock

Mount's Bay Press

First published in 2001 by Mount's Bay Press
Woodland Lodge
Praze-an-Beeble, Camborne
Cornwall TR14 0JE

British Library Cataloguing in Publication Data
A catalogue record for this book is available from the British
Library

ISBN 0-9539991-0-6
Typeset by Amolibros, Watchet, Somerset
This book production has been managed by Amolibros
Printed and bound by T J International Ltd, Padstow, Cornwall,
England

Contents

List of Illustrations

Black and white plates facing page 120

Colour plates facing page 152

Photograph of Rudi and Connie Mock facing page 195

Climate of Cornwall and map, page 94, 95

CHAPTER ONE

Capture

How much do we remember?

Somebody, who has made a study of human behaviour, reckons we recall no more than around 250 dates in a long life. The other days fall like the coppery leaves of autumn – trodden under foot and forgotten. Some dates – some memories – though, stay with us. We never forget them.

On 1st October 1944, I was a member of the Reconnaissance Battalion of the Second Paratroop Army of Germany. We had temporarily taken shelter in a hay barn on the Dutch-German border, licking our bruises from a recent encounter with the 82nd AA American Air Landing Troops near Nymwegen.

Towards the evening, we had a better than normal evening meal and, much to our surprise, the tea was laced with rum and we were allowed to fill our field bottles as well. We soon learned the addition of rum was not to celebrate the commander's birthday, it was a generous helping of Dutch courage in liquid form.

As dusk fell, we all prepared for our next venture.

Ours was a little group with only a non-commissioned officer in charge: an Austrian, he had the look of a man aged about forty-five. He had acquired those last ten years in a matter of a few months, as a member of the 1st Paratroop Army defending Monte Casino, with distinction and near extinction, against the Allied advance in Italy.

We were on reconnaissance, finding out the strength of the opposition, probing the area. Our other objective was to take over a small German village close to the enemy artillery.

How did we feel?

Well there was a strong sense of duty and self-preservation. We were on edge emotionally and, in every sense, at the edge of the unknown.

But we knew we were in experienced hands. We moved towards the Dutch border and, as we approached a farm, a terrible smell met us. I can almost smell that stench today. In the brilliant moonlight, a herd of cows was scattered in the yard, all destroyed, all decaying. We moved quietly in the shadows of the buildings, guarding against the unexpected and, at the same time, hoping to surprise. We had reached our very advanced position and waited for whatever our task was to be. It was the 1st October: the night on which the clocks went back an hour. Our leader kept looking at his watch, everybody was absorbed in his own thoughts. Little did we know the task ahead was big enough to make good use of the extra hour. Finally, the leader raised his arm and we all followed silently, in the traditional German way of parade-ground training, the tallest on the right in parade and the shortest on the far left. At six feet three inches, I was number two. We followed in line, not close enough to come into contact with the man in front, but far enough apart not to present a concentrated target. Suddenly the eerie silence was shattered by intense machine gun cross-fire, the tracers racing from east to west, and west to east at approximately two feet six inches above ground. All hell was let loose.

Without any command, we were all flat on the ground instinctively, and taking stock of our positions. In the clear moonlight we could make out that we were in the middle of a large field, falling towards the enemy. There were several houses in front of us but slightly to the left and right, all in full flame, and a large number of artillery craters all around us. After about five minutes, our corporal indicated with his arm 'forward' but also down. Long basic training had perfected the art of moving forward at reasonable speed without any part of the body ever being more than ten inches above ground. Intermittent machine-gun cross-fire ensured our training instructions were strictly obeyed. We moved this way from crater to crater until a road running parallel in front of the houses separated us from our first target, the few houses not burning on the other side. Intense rifle fire from the house directly in front of us halted our progress.

Our company commander, Ober Feldwebel Wagner, a prospective officer candidate, ordered me to fire my *Panzer Faust*, which I had been delegated to handle. It was a lethal weapon: a hand-held rocket that could knock out a tank.

He ordered me to fire at the house. I took aim and pressed the button. The shell entered the outer wall, some three feet above the ground, leaving a gaping one-foot square hole. I later discovered it had pierced a hole through the next wall as well. I don't know what happened to anybody in that house. It did not concern me, but the firing stopped.

The Ober Feldwebel was standing about a metre to my right, apparently undecided as to what to do next, when he suddenly collapsed without making a sound. I crawled to him. His body felt limp. I felt around his head and found a small amount of warm blood. It was semi-dark; and I could not believe a sniper could see sufficiently well to aim so accurately. To this day, I still wonder if the Americans had night vision.

More than fifty years on, I recall the events of that strange moonlit October night with diamond sharpness. Was it really all those years ago?

Anyway, I felt I could do nothing to help. We were all deeply shocked at the loss of a good leader. I had quietly admired him for the cool, calm way he carried out his responsibilities.

During the next lull of the cross-fire, a very sharp spurt took me across the road to comparative safety for the first time. Several others found their way as well, and I reported to the corporal that Oberfeld Webel Wagner was dead. He told us that Oberfeld Webel Wagner had the signal pistol and an assortment of colours that would indicate our progress. Even if we went back to recover the pistol, we did not know the code. We recovered five severely wounded men from the road, and made them as comfortable as we could in a cellar. Their screams were unbearable. We had no medical supplies; there was nothing we could do. Outside an eerie silence existed and, as the arrangement was, once we had secured the houses on the north side of the road, reinforcements would follow. No signals had gone back and our artillery must have assumed we were in difficulty and a twenty-minute bombardment followed, which we could have done without. The screams from the wounded gradually, after what seemed a lifetime, subsided to whimpers and eventually there was blissful silence. We later checked. Relief had come at last. We were on the ground floor, taking stock of our position: seven of us, no ammunition left, back door secured the best we could. Our group leader decided that someone would have to go outside to investigate our whereabouts.

Any volunteers? No one was mad enough, so it was decided the youngest should go. The night before that would have been my mate Metz, born in 1926. Now, in the morning, it was me. The door was sufficiently opened for me to crawl out. I was well aware of the basic training instructor's first commandment. Never offer your opponent a bigger target than absolutely necessary. So it was flat on your belly, only short movements forward, with elbows working. I make no excuse that I experienced fear as never before or since, investigating an area that had been spitting intense fire at us. The German word 'angst' would properly explain it best. After travelling about twenty feet, I dared to lift my head a little to survey the scene. Some ten metres in front and as far as I could see left and right, was a fence of barbed wire – three rows at the bottom, two at the top and one more at the very top. Lying against the bottom row was one of ours, and another of ours spread-eagled against the top roll of barbed wire. It was an awful sight. I still do not know how they got there, especially the top one, as he could not have climbed there. I can only assume that our own artillery had been responsible.

I felt I had done enough to go back. The way home always appears shorter and quicker.

We came to the conclusion that since we had taken the houses north of the road, there was no more firing by the enemy and therefore we assumed the Americans had withdrawn behind the safety of the barbed wire. We had no means left to defend our position.

It was clear there was no way back over the open ground in daylight. The way forward through, or over, six feet of barbed wire was equally impossible. So it was decided we would wait and see.

After some time, our lookout reported a group of prisoners with roughly forty Americans who had appeared from the right, and our corporal decided we should join them. They were the remnants of our company. A total of perhaps thirty left from our company of one hundred and twenty men. We were all terribly depressed and must have looked a sorry sight. About two hundred metres on our way to what looked like the American headquarters we passed an artillery battery – we realised how lucky we had been. They would have turned us over in our graves at point-blank range.

I was interrogated by a very big American officer. Physically he looked a heavyweight boxer. Our meeting was brief. He would have probed more deeply had I been an officer. I got the impression he knew as much as he wanted to know from the others.

After our short interrogations, we were joined by a major from the infantry. He was caught behind the American lines changing road signs. To us he looked as if he had done a round or two with Mike Tyson. We were taken to a large grass field surrounded with barbed wire where we spent the night with a mixed collection of other prisoners of war.

Later six of us were collected and taken by a British Transport Unit to clean their lorries. One of us had a good command of the English language and when we arrived, the first thing we were asked was, 'Would you like a cup of tea?'

'Of course, we would like a cup of tea. Thank you.'

It was not a cup of tea. It was a mug of tea – and I can still taste it.

That mug of tea was the best drink I've ever had in my life – better than any champagne or the best German wine.

In my experience, the British soldiers respected us. They called us 'Jerries' which was almost a term of affection. They spoke that word because, I believe, they had no contempt for us. They respected ordinary German soldiers and regarded us as honourable fighting men, carrying out our orders – as they were carrying out theirs.

The British Army had spectacular success against the Italians but I don't think that success gave them much satisfaction. We both knew the Italians were not natural soldiers. They did not wear their uniforms with any real pride – and raised the white flag at every opportunity. They surrendered almost happily in hundreds and sometimes thousands.

Next came all those questions soldiers ask each other whenever they meet.

'What unit were you in?'

'How long were you in it?'

'How are your family getting on?'

We showed our family photographs.

There was none of the enmity that you might expect between 'enemies'.

They were doing for their country what was expected of them and we were doing the same for ours. We were down on our luck, and looking back, I suppose these were some of the worst days of my life. Little did I know that events were to shape themselves in such a way that my life would be transformed for the better.

More than half a century later as I sit at my desk working and then wander across to the windows to look out on peaceful green countryside, I realise that but for my capture there on the German-Dutch border my life would have taken a very different course.

People today talk about defining moments in history. Well, in my case, it was a transforming time – but that transformation lay in the thing we call the future. For the present, I was heavily into the grim reality of war – but the future seeds were sown.

Next morning twenty of us were taken by lorry to what turned out to be an American War Cemetery. We were under the supervision of an American. Six of us were delegated to unload any dead Americans as they were brought in from the back of the jeeps and onto a table. We had to remove their boots and empty the contents of their pockets into plastic bags that were marked with their identity. It was interesting to see their expectations of the landing mission. Apart from the normal cigarettes and emergency ration packets, and sometimes bundles of money, many of them had intended to find pleasure. Apart from some very fancy underwear to please the ladies, most had been well equipped to practise safe sex. One ginger-haired American had certainly intended to stay in Europe for a very long time! Tragic as all dead soldiers are, the American noticed, while sealing his bag, that this soldier would have had a problem had he lived. While cigarettes and emergency rations were supposed to be thrown into the dustbin, our guard did not raise any objection if we emptied them first. All dead Americans were wrapped in parachutes before burial.

Our last job for the day was to bury six Germans in the far corner of the cemetery. After placing them in their prepared graves, we observed a minute's silence, giving the military salute over the graves. We were quite sure this had a lasting impression on the two young American guards. On the way back, they appeared deep in thought. Perhaps they drew comparisons, especially if their comrades were unfortunately taller than the standard size of the graves.

Next day we were handed over to the British, and transported to what might have been a nunnery, three per cubicle. We gradually accepted our lot. We were close to the main road and the American supply lorries rolled past day and night. With supplies like this, what hope was there for Germany? We were moved soon again, closer to Ostend, and later into tents and in November, on the wet grass, major problems soon appeared. Dysentery was rampant.

The Allies' earlier hopes of the war being over by Christmas had disappeared and we younger POWs were probably regarded as potentially more dangerous than the older Germans, and, as a result, we were shipped to England. We travelled on a tank landing craft; none of us will forget that wicked cross-channel trip: gale force winds and wild grey seas. Every German prisoner turned his stomach inside out.

We landed at Tilbury and were marched to a greyhound racing stadium. We must have looked a sorry bedraggled sight. We had not had a shave or a wash for six weeks and our rations had been at bare existence level. Now after a refreshing shower, with our clothes cleaned and deloused, we sat down to a light meal and a hot drink – suddenly life was worth living again.

Life is full of curious coincidences. When my name, Mock, was called to collect my package of clothes, an English soldier pressed forward. He could not speak German and I could not speak English but he somehow conveyed the message that he too was called Mock. We shook hands and he offered me a cigarette.

But I did not stay long at Tilbury. Two thousand of us were moved to a camp, previously occupied by American soldiers before their embarkation to Europe. It was near Oswestry; our camp commander was a colonel in the Black Watch, he was a strict but fair man.

Life in those first six weeks as a POW, especially when we were still on the continent, had been no picnic but, looking back and learning later how others had been treated, we had no deep complaints.

Little did I realise in 1942, which was the beginning of the war for me as a soldier, that I should end up a prisoner-of-war.

The start of it was that all men born in 1925 were selected in 1942, at the age of seventeen, for military service. Medical examination established fitness – Class A was fit for everything. Class B was fit for military service, but only suitable for less strenuous duties. Class C was told to go home and come back again next year.

Class A were divided into three groups: airforce, navy and infantry artillery.

On my release from the *Arbeits Dienst* (working services) I had fourteen days' holiday, after which I had to report to the barracks near Nüernberg. There I was fitted with uniform, mess tin and gas mask. All our personal details were recorded and three days later we were off to an unknown destination. The choice of transport was neither first-class nor second-class. It was a traditional transport for soldiers in Germany – a cattle truck with wooden benches round the sides.

The following day we arrived at our destination, which turned out to be La Rochelle in South West France: a climate similar to Cornwall – plenty of rain and plenty of mud on the training fields. The accommodation was a French army barracks, purpose-built. Only the nationality of the occupiers had changed.

Basic training in the German Army was always physically demanding. In the airforce, basic training was used as an assessment for suitability. In January, approximately half of us were selected to go further up near Brest. You were never told where you would go. You just went and did as you were told. Life there was strenuous. There was a small airfield close by and perhaps we served a secondary purpose defending the small airfield. We had to check the identity of anyone coming in and going out and we prepared trenches whenever a general alarm was sounded – which was most nights. The alarm normally lasted from two to six hours. Sometimes you were not more than an hour in bed before the rise-and-shine got us out again. We were certainly toughened up and our training included dealing with unforeseen situations, unexpected obstacles. We only learned much later that this part of our training was mainly for the purpose of selecting non-commissioned officers and fighter pilots – their ability and judgement to deal with the unforeseen was essential. It established your limits and breaking point. One major test was – unknown to us – a morning's very hard exercise wearing gas masks. We were all very close to our limit. A sudden stop-check revealed that two of the men had inserted a small object, like part of a matchstick, between the gas-mask seal and skin. Another had loosened the filter by one turn. Next morning three names were called out to report to the office. We did not know why or what for. On return to the barracks in the evening, the three had disappeared. They had failed the course.

Some were transferred during the course. Approximately half of us, including me, were sent to Graz Talerhof in Austria for training as fighter pilots. Some with academic qualifications were transferred for training as navigators and others with a mechanical background, for training as port mechanics. It was an on-going long process of selection.

It was all now part of Rudi Mock history – and the army had changed my name from Rudolph to Rudi.

CHAPTER TWO

Prisoner-of-war

*L*ife at Camp 8 near Oswestry was more or less in accordance with the Geneva Convention. We were housed in army barracks and fed reasonably well. Boredom was the biggest problem and for those prisoners coming from East Germany there was deep anxiety about families back home being evicted.

The fact that the days were long with little to do was how I first became interested in chess. Cutting out some recognisable figures from whatever could be found was the first step. Then finding a piece of iron that could be sharpened on the grey concrete barrack floor came next. Later we had a piece of good luck: we borrowed a professional blacksmith from a neighbouring barracks. His expertise worked wonders. Iron heated in the bottom of our stove produced much better results.

When some lectures were started, I began learning the English language. It did not come easily to a young man of nineteen, especially the pronunciation, but it helped to fill the hours and, in due course, those of us who persevered made ourselves better understood – and we were able to enjoy a fuller life.

We were not allowed to write home for some time and then only a card with special paper – just to say 'I'm still alive and in England'. It was not until around the middle of April 1945 that we received any news from home, a great time when we finally saw familiar handwriting and read the same lines of news over and over again. Sadly, many prisoners had no news from relatives still in Germany right up to their release in 1948. In their case, no news was almost certainly bad news.

For Christmas 1944, we had a surprise: a £1 gift voucher from the Red Cross to spend in the canteen. Nearly everybody spent it on cigarettes. Those must have been the days for smokers: 160 cigarettes for just one pound. Anything of value was convertible into cigarettes. There was no harder currency than fags: a pullover, sixty, a razor twenty to twenty-five, a badger-hair shaving brush, thirty, and so on. As I had nothing but the clothes I was wearing when taken prisoner, there was plenty for me to barter for – a fountain pen and shaver came next. I never had any desire to smoke and this healthy habit is followed by all our family. It must be in our genes.

The war ended on 5th May 1945.

We prisoners of war felt very depressed. Little was said. When I was first taken prisoner, though things were not going well for us in Europe, there was still some hope. Now that light had gone out.

This was a time of mixed emotions. Of course, there was a degree of relief that all the fighting was over but hopes that we would be released were soon turned to bitter disappointment.

Then came a move – transferred to some camp with an impossible name in South Wales, roughly twenty miles north of Cardiff.

One day, soon after our arrival, an offer was put to some of the prisoners. Those, whose homes were from the area handed over to Poland, could apply to become Polish citizens. The guards at this camp were, in fact, a Polish company. Action was swift. Those prisoners who applied were removed the next day and, a week later, we were surprised to see them, on the other side of the wire, with their rifles guarding over us.

Our new guards looked embarrassed and unhappy and some strong comments flew from our side of the fence: 'You had good. You wanted it better. Don't you wish you had good again?' Another prisoner called out: 'It's no good changing your mind again. We don't want you back.'

Looking at our new uncomfortable guards, men who had been our friends and colleagues a few days ago, I recalled an old saying: 'Don't leave foul water until you have found clean...' It somehow seemed to fit them in their new situation.

It was at this prisoner-of-war camp in South Wales – there were about 4,000 prisoners – that, one morning after our eight o'clock morning roll call, there was a special announcement.

The German manager, acting on decisions made by the senior British officers, announced 600 of us were moving to an 'unknown destination'. Rudi Mock's name was among the 600.

We travelled by train not knowing our route. I remember seeing the sea very close to the railway line near Dawlish in South Devon. Being so close to the sea was something new to me.

Some miles on, the train crossed a narrow bridge above water. The green land beyond looked different, rather like an island. You felt you were leaving the mainland and going to another place.

Eventually, after a long slow journey, we arrived at Lostwithiel and, then carrying all our kit and belongings, marched about three miles to our camp at Par. Of course, we didn't know we were in this place called Cornwall – and names like Par and Lostwithiel only came later on.

Much later did I learn that a man called William Cookworthy, back in the middle of the 1700s, first dug his spade in this land and discovered the minerals which went into the making of the porcelain.

Dame Daphne du Maurier in her book, *Vanishing Cornwall*, wrote of this terrain:

13

'The interest to the layman and to the casual wanderer who finds himself by chance or intention in the china clay country, is the strange, almost fantastic beauty of the landscape, where spoil-heaps of waste matter shaped like pyramids point to the sky, great quarries formed about their base descending into pits filled with water, icy green like arctic pools. The pyramids are generally highest, and the pools deepest, on land which is no longer used; the spoil-heaps sprout grass-seed, even gorse, upon the pumice-stone quality of their surface, and the water in the pits, deeper far than Dozmare, is there because the clay has been sucked off and work begun again on virgin ground.'

Driving towards Bodmin recently and seeing the china clay waste in front of us I said to Connie, my wife, 'Now these pyramids have been levelled off, what do they remind you of?' Without hesitation Connie replied, 'The Table Mountain in Cape Town, South Africa': a very good comparison.

From the camp, we had views of the majestic sweep of St Austell Bay. Later I was to be inspired by another Cornish bay further down the coast. But now I saw little of the bay or the china clay country during the day.

CHAPTER THREE

Rommel

A large number of us were employed in the Army Camp at Bodmin, doing maintenance work, mainly painting doors and windows. I was delegated as an assistant to the cold-storekeeper. Bodmin was a distribution and supply centre for the various military units, which also included the prisoner-of-war camps in Cornwall. My main job consisted of carrying New Zealand lamb wrapped in muslins on to the lorries and keeping the place clean, of course: at the end of the day I had to scrub the wooden chopping block with a wire brush. The storekeeper must have been satisfied with me because he asked for me again the next day, and for the next few weeks we established a good working relationship. The soldier also taught me a few English words, and I like to think that by the time I left he knew the German words for his everyday tools as well. In the first week as POWs we thought the English language was simple, as it consisted only of three extremely rude words. We were quickly made aware that a reply was not necessary as it would only complicate matters. But I should not want the reader to think this indicated any animosity towards us; we engendered indifference at most, and the rude language was part of the soldiers' way of life.

Being a POW has taught us amongst other things that there are many things in life some people can put to good use again, while others would only regard it as waste. I still will not discard things I might find useful later.

Many of us spent a lot of time making children's toys in our camp. Pieces of waste iron were sharpened on the concrete floor to find use as a knife to carve little figures for our chessboards, etc. I used to carve out little doves, secured to a board four at a time with strong cotton and a weight below, a round swinging action pulled the front down, gravity returned them again to their sitting position. Another favourite of mine was a construction of two sticks with a crossbar about halfway down, and strong cotton crossed over at the top and a clown with loosely fixed legs and arms performed all sorts of acrobatics when squeezed at the bottom. My employer at the cold store, whom I regarded by now as a friend, supplied me with the odd empty tea chest; those painting in the army camp supplied the paint, and we were in business. The standard price was two bars of chocolate or fifty Woodbines per toy. We made approximately 300 for local children free of charge for Christmas. It was a very good assortment and of a high standard and a great success as a public relations exercise.

As spring came, more and more of us were employed on local farms, taken out by lorry in the morning and collected in the evening. Generally speaking, the relationship between farmers and POWs was very good and as the farmer wanted it to be. Our packed lunch was very limited in quality and quantity. In most cases the farmers provided a little extra which was always appreciated. The farmer had to pay the full rate based on the time spent on the farm and we received 1.5p per hour according to the time sheet signed by the farmer.

In the spring of 1946, we were moved again to smaller camps, close to the farms where we were to be employed, like Clowance near Praze, or Helston, or St Erth for me. The beauty of Cornwall impressed me immediately, immensely.

It was a beautiful spring day, my first sight of Mount's Bay, blue and inviting, the tide in and St Michael's Mount cut off from the mainland. It all combined to make a picture almost too beautiful to be true – the kind of setting you might expect to see on a cinema screen or in a great work of art. This was another world from the china clay country and Bodmin Moor and towns like Lostwithiel and St Austell.

I was looking at what I later learned was 'the golden square mile', the Gulval area just outside Penzance which is the richest horticultural land in all Cornwall. Farmers in the roadside fields were harvesting cauliflowers that would not have survived the winter at Par. I have seen many lovely places in various parts of the world but no other place has made such an impression. Immediately I felt in tune with the place.

Our destination was St Erth Camp, just outside the village of St Erth, which is about halfway between the narrowest point of Cornwall between Hayle and Marazion. The closeness to the sea, north and south, and the Gulf Stream makes the area still most suitable for horticulture or out of season crops. We worked almost exclusively on local farms in ones, twos and threes, returning to the camp in the evening. I spent nearly all my time working on the same farm – South Trewennack, near St Hilary. The traditional extra for lunch was fried potatoes and egg, or something similar, served with a smile by the farmer's daughter. There was occasional overtime paid at half a crown net. Considering the normal pay was one and a halfpence per hour this was very welcome. As the traditional farm-workers were returning home from the war, these small outlying camps were closed and we were transferred to the main camp at St Columb.

I then had a spell of six months on a dairy farm at Trencrom, living in as family. I had a good room and lived with the family. The lady of the house was a widow, the eldest son a bachelor of probably forty-five years in age, his eldest sister a year or two younger, another sister, and of course me. We had one thing in common – we were all unattached and independent, an odd collection. Trencrom Farm was a rented dairy farm, a hard farm, full of rocks. The farmer's highlight of the week was a visit to St Ives with his sister in his little Austin 8, to listen to the Salvation Army Band.

I remember one Sunday evening it was raining cats and dogs when he said to his sister, 'Lottie, do you want to go to St Ives tonight?'

A quick look out of the window and her reply was, 'I think I will give it a miss tonight.'

'Well, if you are not coming I don't think I shall take the car,' was Wilfred's reply. Off he went, walking some six miles to St Ives. I did not have the benefit of seeing what he looked like when he came home. I must have been in bed asleep for some hours. I don't think he had any other great demands on life. In the evenings after our meal he sat in his old chair directly under the wireless, one eye closed and the other half open, listening to the news, looking blissfully happy and content.

Soon after my arrival, one Sunday evening, I went for a walk up Trencrom Hill, a well-known local landmark. It is only a little hill but it rises up sharply, close to the edge of the granite area of Penwith – the local name for this westerly part of Cornwall. It is a perfect natural fort with steep sides and folklore has it that treasure is buried here guarded by ugly spriggans who, when any treasure hunters appear, rise howling and menacing from the grey rocks. So the treasure remains. That anyway is the tale the old folks told.

On my return, I met a neighbour and his wife who had been attending to their beehives nearby. We struck up a good conversation. The man was curious to know what made us tick.

He then asked me, 'Do you play chess?'

'A little,' I replied and, as a result, I was invited to their house.

We started our first game on a proper board with proper pieces. He chose white and started with an aggressive line that soon proved over-optimistic. The second game was played with more thought and lasted about thirty minutes. His wife served a good cup of coffee and excellent cake.

I later learned that Mrs Harvey regularly swept the board in the local village show for her baking, bottling and honey exhibits. Refreshed, we started game number three. The play was now in earnest and I also had some serious thinking to do. This was not bad for a POW and I did not intend to spoil it. We had a good game and after some time I decided to offer a draw. Honours were saved.

As I was about to leave, Mr Harvey explained, 'I'm the secretary of the chess club in Lelant, which includes members from Penzance and St Ives, and our chess club meets on Monday evenings. Would you like to come with me on Monday evening?'

Of course, I did. But what sort of reception would I get? I had always imagined chess players would be stuck-up and snobs – or eggheads – and that turned out to be completely wrong.

You could not find a nicer cross-section of the community, gentlemen to the core. As I am shy by nature, and have no knowledge of the niceties of protocol, the first Monday evening was a big challenge. Anyway, I was made very welcome. The club members ranged from Captain Napier, member of a well-known Scottish family, his wife, daughter of the famous Cornish Bolitho family, whose name is still over the door of Barclays Bank in Penzance, her sister, a bank manager from St Ives, the director and owner of Carbis Bay Hotel in St Ives, the headmaster of a local school, a schoolteacher, an engineer, my new-found friend, Mr Harvey, the railway station master, a council road man and a ship steward. Our first match was a friendly against the Royal Marines training in St Ives. At the recommendation of the club secretary, I took his place and played on the bottom board no 6. The marines were obviously much better at climbing cliffs than playing chess and we won 6-0. Had they invited us to a cliff-climbing competition in return, the result would have been worse for us! I do not know what the marines thought of the man with funny patches on his uniform, but I expect somebody put them right.

Where and when and by whom chess was invented, all remain unsolved mysteries. But we do know that chess is an ancient game, probably about a thousand years old. References to a form of chess appear in the literatures of ancient Egypt, Rome and Greece.

I learnt my chess, as a prisoner-of-war, in barracks but times were when it was a pastime of royal families and nobility; as time advanced, though, the middle classes became involved, the prosperous merchants and the professional classes joining the ranks of chess players.

This may account for the fact that the world of chess has been peopled by so many colourful characters. The truth is chess is no dull-as-dust pastime and those who play it are artists – great or small. The history of chess is a kind of mirror reflecting social history.

The emergence of chess in Europe and later, across the Atlantic, in the United States was all bound up with the development of trade routes and historical events like the Crusades.

I do not pretend to have been a great player but chess opened doors for me into Cornish homes and families – and I am grateful for that fact.

The greatest glory in my chess career came a few years later. Cornwall played regularly in the South West league, usually at Exeter University on a Saturday afternoon. Cornwall was always short of willing good players and this occasion one of our chosen club members could not make it. I was asked if I would replace him. I knew very well my play was not up to county standard, but reluctantly accepted. To lose one point by default would not be any better than losing over the board.

I think I was chosen to play on board 14 out of 20 and my opponent was a student from Bristol University who had the advantage of playing white. My heartbeat was on overtime, especially as he chose an aggressive opening. My style was generally defensive, waiting for the opponent to make the mistake. All his pieces were in an attacking position. I had very little hope of withstanding such a massive attack without losing material. I'm not normally a slow player but my clock was ticking away for ten minutes when I suddenly realised a move with my Knight gave his Queen just one place in which to move. My heartbeat was even more irregular when I realised my other Knight could fork his King and Queen with the same move. My opponent could not even retake the offending piece as some compensation. Without a Queen and threatening more losses, there was no hope for him. The offer of a handshake acknowledged defeat. A chess room is normally like a morgue – dead quiet. So when both of us stood up, all heads turned. A county game finished after only thirty minutes play out of three hours was a sensation. I tried to avoid our team captain's eye but when I finally stuck my thumb up, his face changed completely. I was under pressure to play again. I knew very well I could not be that lucky again, and did not yield. Pressure of work was a genuine reason, but to hold 100 per cent record of success playing for the county cannot be claimed by many either.

I looked forward to my Monday evenings and I became an established player in the team. Gradually I worked my way up to no 5 board, and later to no 4, with a national grading of 146, which is about the middle in an average league team playing for the Cornish Shield. The League Club won this shield in my first year. For the rest of my stay at Trencrom Farm I spent most evenings with the Harveys. Mr Harvey had a wood-turning lathe in his garden shed. We spent endless hours making a chess set. Mr Harvey did the turning of the lathe and my job was the carving, like the Knights and the other pieces. The final polishing was done with beeswax. We were very proud of our completed set.

I have many happy memories of those chess-playing evenings and matches, often a privilege because POWs were not expected to go further than one mile from the base.

When our team played Padstow in North Cornwall, I was included. My friend, Mr Harvey, a great fixer, found for me somebody with a good suit he had outgrown. I see the donor occasionally in Camborne and I believe now, fifty years later, the suit would still fit. I was invited by Captain Napier and his family for Sunday tea: a great honour, especially as Captain Napier still suffered with breathing difficulties after having been gassed in World War One. It just shows ordinary people do not cause wars, or are at war with each other. They are just the ones who pay the price.

Around this time I was considering staying over here as a civilian for another year. Our release was expected later in 1948 and the British government had decided that about 20,000 German POWs could apply to stay on in the United Kingdom.

Two of my POW friends, working on a farm near Hayle, said, 'We're thinking of staying on for another year. Why don't you join us, Rudi?'

I had already been thinking of doing just that. Anyway I discussed the matter with my good friend Mr Harvey and, as a result of that conversation, he drove me in his little Austin 7 to see Mr Walter Eddy, a gentleman farmer, who owned as many as three farms in the area.

'Rudi's a good member of our chess club,' Mr Harvey explained, 'and we want to keep him.'

Mr Eddy was agreeable to the idea and a formal contract was signed by him, the camp authorities and me. The great advantage was I became a civilian, entitled to the full agricultural wage of £4.10s for a forty-eight-hour week.

Mr Eddy was indeed a gentleman farmer. The only time I saw him doing any manual work was sowing the spring cabbage on Saturday mornings in July. Maybe he liked to keep his hand in or perhaps he didn't trust anybody else to do that. The farm concentrated on broccoli, spring cabbage and early potatoes. We three Germans lived in a primitive farm-workers' cottage on the land. We appreciated that he gave us overtime at half a crown net. This was a valuable addition, enabling us to purchase extra clothing coupons from a fellow workman with a large family. It also meant we could send the occasional parcel to the family back home in Germany where things were scarce and life difficult.

There was, of course, inside all of us POWs, a deep desire to go home and see our families. The British government, to their credit, understood this desire and generously gave us free travel papers, from door to door and back again. We travelled by train, the compartments all occupied by Germans. That train journey ensured that in 1948, at least, Father Christmas was coming not from Lapland but from England.

I had left my mother in the autumn of 1943. She had a full head of black hair. Now her hair was as white as the snow that covered the landscape outside. My brother had returned from Italy, where he too had been a POW, and there were tears of joy over the family reunion.

The village had been barely touched by the war in terms of damage to property. Ironically, an American tank coming through it had fired a single shot and this went straight through my bedroom window – the only damage sustained in the entire village.

But, overall, our homeland was in a terrible state: massive destruction, especially in the cities. With the expulsion of approximately six million people from the territories handed over to Poland, there was chaos. These people were allowed to bring with them only what they could carry. Starvation, sickness and death were everywhere. No doubt we were in the best place here in Cornwall.

The big question is, 'Could the war have ended earlier?'

It was in May 1941 that Rudolf Hess, Hitler's deputy, made an extraordinary decision.

Intending, as he wrote in his last letter to Hitler, 'to risk my life to make peace and end bloodshed', Hess ordered a Messerschmitt 110 to be fitted with auxiliary petrol tanks and took off from Augsburg, parachuting from the plane at Eaglesham near Glasgow, in Scotland. He was arrested and kept in prison for the rest of his life, his peace terms ignored.

This incredible mission led to people asking questions – more than fifty years later they remain unanswered questions. Did Hitler know about it beforehand? Did Churchill? How did he fly his plane so expertly and not get shot down? Was there a peace party in Britain that was expecting him?

The whole episode is like something out of a novel – not real life.

Andrew Roberts, writing in the *Mail on Sunday* in April 1999, had this to say:

'...the story has joined the identity of Jack the Ripper and the truth about the *Mary Celeste* as one of our most popular mysteries. There are other unexplained events in the Second World War – why did Hitler stop his tanks outside Dunkirk, for example, and why did Germany declare war on America? But they are usually serious and strategic rather than personal and weird.

'Of all the theories that have been produced about the "mission", one of the strangest was that put forward by the former British Army surgeon Dr Hugh Thomas, who had examined the man incarcerated in Berlin's Spandau prison after the Nuremberg Trials and who sensationally claimed he was not Rudolf Hess at all, but a schizophrenic impostor who had been substituted.

'A bullet wound Hess received in the First World War had disappeared, as had a gap between his front teeth that was evident in photos of 1941 but not in those of 1945.

'This theory was comprehensively mocked by responsible historians but, if the state has no secrets still to hide about the mission, why does it not release all the files now?'

An interesting postscript to the whole Hess saga concerns an American writer called Eugene Bird. An American Colonel, Eugene Bird, first met Hess when he was part of the garrison at Spandau Gaol, a fortress built to house six hundred where Hess was the sole prisoner. Later, as Commandant, he won Hess's confidence to such a degree that he was able to keep a day-to-day record of the conversations.

The result was a book entitled *The Loneliest Man in the World, Rudolf Hess in Spandau* (published first by Martin Secker and Warburg in 1974 and later published as a paperback in 1980 by Sphere Books).

Here is what Colonel Bird wrote in his epilogue to that book:

'In early March 1972 I had been to the United States where I had left my wife, Donna, seriously ill, continuing with her medical treatment. On the way back, I had called into Washington where I spent some days in the Archives building going over the Hess File and copying the Hess-Haushofer letters.

'I was putting my key into the door of our Fischottersteig, Berlin, home when the phone began to ring. It was Donna from Florida. There had been a strange telegram from my Berlin superior officer, asking when I was likely to return. "It sounds odd, Gene," she said.

'I put down the phone and then called Spandau Prison to talk to Warder Donham, the man I had left in charge. He sounded strangely stiff and formal. He assured me all was well with the prisoner and that Hess had been missing me. But there was none of our previous easy-going relationship. I felt uneasy.

'Next morning I drove through the slush of winter Berlin to the US Mission Headquarters and went to the office of my superior, Mr Small. He said: "Gene, I have some questions for you and I want them answered." There were tapes in existence concerning Rudolf Hess which had been taped inside the prison. There was also, he understood, a manuscript which had been written with Rudolf Hess's full co-operation. Only one man was close to Hess. Had I been responsible?

'I told him yes, I had.

'I was then interrogated for several hours. I was allowed to go home but placed under house arrest. My house was kept under 24-hour surveillance, my phone was tapped, a team of officers came and made a thorough search of every room. They took away documents, letters, photographs and negatives dating back to 1934. Every page was then laboriously cross-indexed with the information which appears in this book. I was allowed to travel about Berlin in my car, but when I did, three cars, each containing two Secret Service men, followed.

'I was put under oath when I made the following statement...before the US flag and a portrait of the US President, and I was asked to resign my job as US Commandant of Spandau. This I did. I was also made to sign a Secrets Act, a documents I, as a retired Army officer, had not signed before.

'Later in Washington, while staying at the same hotel from which the Watergate raids were made, I went before a Board of State Department officials. Sitting opposite me I recognised with some amusement the man who had flown to Berlin and asked me if, for the sake of the US historical record, I might be able to persuade Rudolf Hess to divulge his secrets before he died. (I had told him I would do my best.)

'They told me that several copies of the 160,000-word manuscript had been made. One was being kept in a sealed vault, another was sent to the Department of the Secretary of State, a third was with the Department of the Secretary of Defence, a fourth was in the Archives in Washington, and one had been sent to the office of the US Commander, Berlin. Again I smiled to myself. It was this same gentleman's Chief of Staff, who had been reading my manuscript, chapter by chapter, from the time it was three-parts completed. He had even allowed his wife to read it. Both had told me it was "terrific" and all had offered several constructive suggestions to add to its scope. The Director of the Archives in Berlin had been allowed by me to read it as it was written, and so had several other officers. In short, if it had not been the subject of conversation in the general officers' mess and at the officers' wives' bridge parties I would have been surprised indeed.

'But now I was going through questioning and rebukes by men who, if the US Secret Service has efficiency at all, must have known about my book's production for years and had done nothing whatsoever to stop its compilation.

It told them that they must have realised there was nothing in it which breached any secrets act; nothing that could be used against the US by a future enemy. I believed – and they should agree – that it was an important and unique historical document. They said nothing other than I would have to wait their permission to publish it.

'I told them its publication might well do something that the Heads of State of Britain, the United States and France all wanted, but had failed to achieve: force the Russians to bow to the weight of sheer public opinion and release Hess.

'This I believe could happen as millions around the world read for the first time the true story of the old man's incarceration for year after year purely because a country is using him as a political pawn for its own ends.

'Only the future will tell.'

The war produced some truly historic figures on both sides. On our side Field Marshal Rommel was a military genius.

He was one of the great commanders of the war, highly regarded by his men and the enemy. Outside and beyond his military leadership, there were those in Germany who hoped for a separate peace with the west – and Rommel was seen as the best ambassador capable of leading such a delegation and negotiating such a peace plan.

Dr John Pimlott, who edited the volume *Rommel, In His Own Words* (published by Greenhill Books in 1994), reflected:

'This appears to have contributed to his downfall, for many members of the July 1944 Bomb Plot clearly regarded Rommel as a possible leader of post-Nazi Germany, with special emphasis on negotiations with the West. His direct involvement in the Bomb Plot is difficult to prove. Although by 1944 he had lost faith in the Nazi leadership, blaming Hitler's entourage for a series of strategic miscalculations in North Africa and Italy, there is little evidence that he was aware of the intention to assassinate the Fuhrer and would almost certainly had disassociated himself from the attempt. But the mere mention of his name in the interrogations of key prisoners was enough to seal his fate. By then Hitler was convinced that he had lost the loyalty of the German Officer class and was prepared to believe any rumour of association with the plotters that emerged.'

On 14th October 1944 two German generals visited Rommel. They told him his name had been discovered in a conspirators' document naming him as Hitler's successor. The generals went on to tell Rommel he was deeply suspected of being involved in the plot to kill Hitler.

The field marshal was given two grim alternatives. Either he consumed poison or he would be stripped of his distinguished military rank and charged before a people's court. They informed him if he took the former course then his family would be safe.

Rommel told his family of his decision. He drove away in a staff car with the two generals. Only a mile on, the car pulled up and Rommel 'took the poison'. His body was taken to Ulm and the official announcement was made: 'Field Marshal Rommel has died of a brain haemorrhage...'

Such are the curious twists and turns of history.

CHAPTER FOUR

A Visit to Germany,
Back to Cornwall and Connie

*1*948 was a year of revaluation of the currency in Germany: everyone lean and hungry, raring to go. My job in the office resembled a firm like Farm Industries here in Cornwall: selling everything the farmer needs and buying back his harvest. It was not the kind of work I wanted. Without a grammar-school education, I had little hope of promotion but it was a job – and that in the Germany of 1948 was something. Many young men in my shoes would have been thankful but I was ambitious.

My aim was to work hard and reap the benefits. I did not plan to work hard and make somebody else rich and I manoeuvred accordingly, going to see the personnel director at headquarters.

I was assured my job was safe and I was given a generous Christmas gratuity.

'What will happen,' I asked,'if I return to England for another year and see how the situation in Germany has settled after revaluation?'

'Your job will still be here for you.'

Over a cup of coffee, he and his wife asked me all sorts of questions about England. Their son was a POW in the North of England where he was removing mines.

'He is coming to visit us in January,' they told me, 'but he is considering returning to England.'

We parted as friends and, more important, I had not burnt my bridges.

I have a vivid memory of that visit – meeting an old lady on the footpath just outside the village with a candle and rosary in her hand. She was the mother of my best friend. His name is on the war memorial: Muller Franz 13–7–1944. I knew where she was going. We spoke only a few words before we were both overcome with emotion. There were many mothers and wives over there feeling exactly the same – likewise British mothers and wives – grief on both sides of the Channel.

I returned to England convinced that one day I would work for myself, possess my own house, get married and raise a family – ideally, in that order, but not necessarily so. One of the three POWs did not return from Germany. His mother was in a terrible state, having lost everything in the East, and being unable to fend for herself. He could not leave her by herself. Fortunately, another friend of mine was looking for a job down here in Cornwall and three of us living together would be easier than two – especially as he was a good friend. The other two had girlfriends, but I was in no hurry. An introduction to one mate's girlfriend's sister did not whet my appetite.

There were girls from the Land Army working on Mr Eddy's farm and I noticed one tall good-looking girl from London called Connie. She was often skylarking about and though you couldn't call it love at first sight – I was a shy young man – I hoped we would get to know one another.

It was the start of the football season and I discovered something called 'the football pools' and how to take part in this game of chance where an ordinary working man or woman may suddenly join the ranks of the rich. I say 'suddenly' because it all depended on what happened during ninety minutes on Saturday afternoon. Thousands of people stopped whatever they were doing to listen to the football results on the radio – we called it the wireless in those days – writing down the results and checking them against their coupons. Win or lose, there was a bit of excitement in the air for a few minutes.

For some people, like betting on horses, it became a disease and they squandered too much. I had no intention of catching that disease but I resolved to have a flutter and turned to Fred, our tractor driver, for his words of wisdom on the subject.

Fred explained, 'You'll find more home wins than away wins or draws.'

The pools promoters had invented interesting titles like Favourite Four, Easy Six or Eight Draws. Easy Six? If you believed that, then you believed in Father Christmas.

Where is the Arsenal? Manchester United? Aston Villa? Such names might have been on the other side of the moon, but on this first Saturday of the season only the Scottish clubs were playing. Difficult decisions. Down went my four home wins under Favourite Four. All my four teams scored goals and won their matches – and Littlewoods sent me a postal order for 7s 6d by return post.

The other farm-workers didn't win a sausage.

On the strength of this win, I plucked up courage to speak to Connie.

'Would you like to go to the pictures in Penzance on Saturday evening?'

It took me the best part of ten minutes to say those thirteen words.

Connie recalls, 'I was surprised when he asked me out and I made sure he didn't pick me up at the hostel just outside Penzance because I knew all the other girls would be watching.'

I can still see her coming towards the railway station, our agreed meeting point. It was the first time I had seen Connie out of her wellies and dungarees. With her measuring six feet and me six feet three inches, I had found a matching partner. The following week, on a visit to Mr Uren, the local dentist, he said he was also in the queue and complimented me on how well matched we were.

Perhaps, in many ways we are. Her full name is Constance. It is very appropriate; and, as well as being reliable and honest, she is easy to get on with. Her father died when she was three and a half, mine when I was four years old. So, neither of us were spoiled or likely to make unreasonable, unobtainable demands on life. After the pictures, we had fish and chips and there was a little change left. Connie had to be back in the prefabricated camp by eleven p.m. and I had to catch the last bus to Hayle at ten-thirty. But we were both pleased with our first outing.

More than fifty years on, those Saturday night dates remain vivid memories. The farm on which I worked was about a mile outside Hayle. I'd cycle into the town, put my bike in the car park behind the White Hart Hotel and catch the bus to Penzance. Sometimes, after the film, I missed that last green bus and had to walk the eight up-and-down miles to Hayle. One night, deep in thought, I walked all the way back to the farm only to realise that I had forgotten the bike at the White Hart, so had to walk back into town to collect it.

The lifestyle of us three Germans sharing a cottage, though, was soon to be shattered. One day, on the way with Fritz to meet his girlfriend's family, he pointed out a fact of life I had not previously considered – that some men only had to hang their trousers on the bedpost to bring themselves endless trouble. My fears were confirmed in less than a quarter of an hour for his trousers must have been hanging there for some time. So we now had a problem. Where could they live? My other friend Erich and his girlfriend planned to marry at Easter and a tied cottage on the farm was available to them. It was not a palace, but a lick of paint and new wallpaper made it quite acceptable and it was rent-free. That left Fritz with the other cottage where we were living. The option to live with either of them was on offer but it did not fit in with my long-term plans to gain experience and one day start growing flowers on my own.

There was only one serious shadow during my time with Mr Eddy. One morning we were having 'crib', the Cornish expression for a mid-morning break and something to eat, when his son, Walter Eddy Junior, asked, 'What's this game of chess you play, Rudi?' I got the impression that he might like to take it up but we never had the chance to discuss it again. Later that day he was killed in a lorry crash on his way back from the station. I attended the funeral service at Ludgvan Church. It was packed with hundreds of people – and emotion – the biggest funeral service I have ever attended. Clearly, he was a very popular young man.

Other than that one sad episode, I enjoyed my time with Mr Walter Eddy. He was good about overtime but did not like his men working on a Sunday. In my two years there, we did work on only one Sunday – baling hay. On balance though, I thought it was time to move on; so the accommodation problem was a good reason or excuse to do just that.

The *West Briton* newspaper, in certain parts of Cornwall, is the Cornishman's Bible and, one Thursday evening, looking through it, an advertisement caught my eye: 'An assistant required in a small market garden to grow vegetables and flowers for the Hotel and the surplus will be sold in Truro. Accommodation provided.' I applied and came the reply, 'Come and see how you like it. Unless you are happy with your job no good work can be done.'

Thus I handed in my notice, explaining my reasons and thanking Mr Eddy for having been a good employer for me. The explanation to my mates was that I did not feel happy to impose on them, and felt that newly weds should be left alone. I had stayed long enough to be best man at Fritz's wedding. The other witness was a friend of the bride – a midwife: prudent thinking.

My new place of employment was at Ruan High Lanes on the Roseland Peninsula, which has a sub-tropical climate. The Roseland, like the Lizard further south, is a kingdom of its own. There is a strong Cornish quality about the area, names like Gerrans and Portscatho, Veryan and Treluggan. Oddly enough, the word Roseland has nothing to do with flowers. I later learned it came from an old Celtic word Rhos – which means heath or gorse.

Roseland is certainly the last place you would associate with a violent unsolved murder case. But that lay half a century into the future.

Then I was looking for more experience on the land and Major Reeves' position fitted my long-term plans. I wanted to learn more about flowers – was hungry for knowledge.

A very nice room was provided and all meals were taken in the kitchen. The food was the same for the guests, the major's family and staff. The only exception was Friday evening meal, the changeover for the guests, and salmon was on the menu. At £1 a pound the major did not have any either.

The only big disadvantage of the new working arrangement was that Connie and I were a long way apart but we had known each other long enough that I felt we had a future together and was confident she felt the same. She was aware of my ambitions, understood a job like my new one was, for the time being, necessary. We continued to meet regularly on Saturday afternoons in Truro. Well, as the saying goes, 'Absence makes the heart grow fonder.' We wrote to each other once a week. Connie is much the better letter writer. I always suspected that I was slightly dyslexic so she had the benefit of longer enjoyment deciphering my letters.

I enjoyed my job, a little bit of everything. A large variety of vegetables were grown, and, much to my delight, some anemones for the market. It is a crop that can only be grown in West Cornwall for it flowers from September to the following April. Nowadays it is far less used for commercial purposes; its genetic make-up has declined and it no longer tolerates the colder climates that it used to. Stock, polyanthus and kaffir lilies were the other flowers grown. In my mind, I was beginning to see the future.

One of my jobs was to milk the two house cows in the morning and evening. Major Reeves' daughter Jane, who had an agricultural education, was still recovering from polio, and gave me strict instructions on how to feed them. So much of this, so much of that, a little bit of this and that, and walking away, she said casually, 'And this one, Bella is in the habit of kicking.' I milked the other cow first, and I was rather pleased with the bucketful of milk. Bella was next. It had to be done. Protecting the bucket as much as I could with my legs, I soon discovered the problem was only with one teat. It was what I call a pea in that teat. It was not for me to know why it was there, or what caused it. The more usual way of stripping the teats wasn't going to be possible, so I squeezed the milk out avoiding this tender spot as best I could. With two full buckets of milk, I was rather pleased with myself. As I opened the door, there was Jane, grinning from ear to ear. I had an idea that she was not far away and I did not know who was more pleased, Jane, myself or Bella. After this, I couldn't do wrong. When I told Dick, the foreman, he told me he wouldn't milk that 'so-and-so' cow, and since the former milking girl had left, the neighbouring farmer came over and milked her.

The cook and his wife left for Australia, and an ex-captain quartermaster begged the major for temporary employment, desperately needing a roof over his head. His wartime marriage had just broken down and he was destitute. George turned out to be a smashing bloke. One morning, when I had to wake Jane to ask for the cow house keys, I saw George's little head peeping out from under the blankets. Clearly, Jane was of the same opinion.

Jane was quite an attractive girl, and, most important, always made you feel at home. She later married a doctor and produced twins, an achievement which prompted her mother to say, 'Trust Jane to do the extraordinary!' Mrs Reeves, I believe, had been a professional dancer in India where she had met her husband.

The major was a liaison officer in the United States during the war and, as a result, we had a number of American visitors. He was a cautious man. I remember sometimes when driving downhill, he would turn off the engine – to save petrol.

When I moved into my room in the hotel I was told that in high season it would be needed for paying guests and then I could share the old coach house with two others or, as an alternative, there would be a large tent in the garden. I chose the large tent, preferring to be on my own.

Also employed at the hotel were a recently married couple, working for their keep and experience only. He was a waiter and his young wife a chambermaid.

One night their bed collapsed and, next morning, she appeared at breakfast with a broad grin on her face. 'That's not why it happened!' she explained. The major, like Queen Victoria, was not amused.

After a short time, the same young lady, in a highly agitated state, produced some startling news: 'My husband has left me…and for good!'

Later that night she came to my tent and enquired, 'Rudi, may I borrow your push bike?'

I formed the impression she was looking for somewhere to sleep and someone perhaps with whom to sleep. Though she was an attractive red-haired young woman, I was due to be married and simply replied, 'Of course, you can borrow my cycle. You know where it is.'

Next morning I looked at my cycle. It was obvious she had not used it. My intuition was correct: she wanted rather more than my 'push bike'.

Major Reeves' business was too small for him to make a fortune but his thriftiness went a long way to saving one. He took on some staff looking for experience and a good reference at the end of it – just for their keep. Life was never dull and I enjoyed my stay there – and all the time I was gaining more and more practical experience.

The Women's Land Army dissolved and now Connie took a temporary job as a nursemaid at St Hilary: a living-in post.

We were now thinking about marriage and this brought a big question.

'Where do we live?'

The solution came through a curious coincidence. I had a friend John, a fellow POW from North West Germany, down in West Cornwall working on a farm at St Erth run by Mr and Mrs Wilfred Harry. We had kept in contact and I decided to write to him asking, 'If and when that farm cottage down there becomes vacant, will you please let me know?'

Incredibly, our letters crossed in the post.

He wrote, 'There is a vacancy here and the farm cottage has become vacant. Would you be interested in it?'

Of course, we were interested. It had the look of an ideal country cottage with roses around the door. There were three bedrooms, a kitchen, a sitting room and a living room.

People said, 'You lucky so-and-so!'

The major was not particularly pleased but, in my heart, I knew the time had come to move on again.

We were lucky but there was a price to pay. It was a tied cottage – which meant no rent – but I had to work two weekends out of three, helping to milk about thirty cows by hand.

On the first day of May, the farmer and his wife came to collect me. The arrangement was that I would live in the cottage but would have meals with the farmer and his family and my German friend. Connie liked the whole pattern because she lived just two miles away.

One week, on her day off, Connie arrived at the farm in an excited state. 'I've spotted a three-piece suite in a furniture store in Causewayhead, Penzance, for £35 in a sale. Imitation leather, soft seats…a real bargain!'

I did not disappoint her. Her wages were always low and she sent ten shillings every week to her mother in London where rents were high. My savings, over the last three years, had found good use.

In our free time we painted and decorated, getting ready for the big day in November. Looking back, it was fun adding bits and pieces to the cottage, step-by-step. We agreed right from the beginning that we would never borrow money for anything that was for our personal use – and we have stuck by that policy to this very day. To borrow money for business was a different matter – and even then it was always short-term.

There is a romance about cottages. Many paintings depict cottages and they have long been much-loved, much-photographed subjects. The Cornish writer Derek Tangye wrote a whole string of books about his life in a cottage on the cliffs near Lamorna on the other side of Penzance.

This cottage of ours at St Erth looked a dream from the outside but there was little romance inside its four walls.

Like so many Cornish cottages of that time, rising damp or dampness kept coming through the wall, especially from the west side. In the living room, we added a fifteenth layer of wallpaper to the others already there. The cooking and lighting was by calor gas. Water had to be fetched from across the road. Rainwater collected in a tank provided washing water; dipping the washbowl in the tank on a frosty morning soon woke you up. The toilet was up the garden path – all right when you are young, but not so good later in life. These facilities were common for farm-workers in the late 1940s and the early 1950s. A nice garden was an attraction. It was too small for the tractor and plough so I did it all by shovel. I was fit and able in those days. We planted 10,000 anemones, some white pinks and some grape hyacinths. Connie helped with the planting. Weeds were not allowed to live.

Connie picked the flowers during the daytime and we bunched them in the evening. I packed them before we went to work and the farmer took them to the station when he took the milk to the factory. He was very helpful.

The farmer Wilfred Harry, my boss, was a great football fan. He supported the Magpies; the Penzance football team wore black and white – so the name was inevitable. The Cornish, I discovered, are very superstitious, especially the older people in those days. They never liked seeing a single magpie. That solitary bird was regarded as a bad omen but the sighting of two magpies indicated good luck. I think football was just about the biggest part of Wilfred Harry's life. He would stand on the halfway line and shout 'Come on the Magpies!' Or he would shout support for an individual player. He was a great supporter of Charlie Sutherley, the powerful Penzance winger who had played for Exeter as a young man.

The most famous Magpie of that time was Gerry Gazzard who played inside left. Gerry had wonderful ball control and dribbled so skilfully that you felt the ball was tied to his left boot with an invisible piece of string. He went on to play professional football for the London club West Ham.

In time the Magpies moved from St Clare, where they shared with the cricket club, to a ground of their own called Penlee Park, near the sea front. Mr Harry, with the aid of his farm tractor and his two daughters, helped to level the pitch at Penlee Park before the Magpies started their first season there.

The Harrys rented their farm from a wealthy West Cornwall landowner, Lord St Levan, who lived in his castle at the top of St Michael's Mount in Mount's Bay. Originally, the Harrys farmed one of the St Levan's properties near Land's End. The farm was close to the radio mast there – a very important mast, the first in the United Kingdom. Consequently, it attracted the attention of German bombers during the war. So much so that Lord St Levan said, 'I've a safer farm further inland near St Erth…if you'd like to rent that one, you can have it.' And that's how they came to Tredrea Farm, just outside St Erth on the Marazion road.

We never saw Lord St Levan of course. He left dealings with his tenant farmers to his agent.

Quite important things happened in 1951. The Conservatives, under Winston Churchill, came back into power. In October, King George VI underwent a major operation. In February, in Australia, the England cricketers won their first test match against their old cricketing rivals since the 1930s. Marilyn Monroe had just made a film called *All About Eve* and I had an important date.

We got married at St Michael's Church, Harlesden in North West London in the November.

Those were the days of ration books, many things still scarce, but Connie's mother and aunt made it a nice family affair.

We returned to Cornwall by night train to our cottage, our new home for the next five years – and married life.

St Erth then was essentially quiet farming countryside. Buses were important because many families did not own a motor car. St Erth Station was – and remains – a terminus of the St Ives branch line. The lanes in and around St Erth were narrow, often twisting; consequently cars using them travelled slowly – when measured against the motoring speeds of today. The village houses and cottages were the homes of local working people – not holiday homes or the residences of commuters. Many farms were small, run by generations of the same family. Village post offices and village stores generally flourished.

On our first Boxing Day, a terrific gale blew down a large tree on an adjoining unused piece of land. I cut it to handy-sized pieces. The farmer lent us his tractor and circular saw and my friend helped me to cut it into logs. We had no need to purchase any coal for all the years we were at Tredrea. Grateful for the wood, the farmer was happy to let me use this piece of land once I had cleaned it up. My friend ploughed it and cultivated it for me. This was a place where there had been straw and hayricks for many years, and the waste created a rich humus soil, ideal for anemones. Our first-year flowers had not yet finished and brought us a net income of £150. In the following year, we planted 30,000 anemones in the new piece of land. The shelter around provided ideal conditions and again top-quality blooms. With the net income in that year of in excess of £350 we were making progress: better than my yearly wages.

We were living on my wages. I got £6 a week. What we made on our sideline – the flowers – we saved. Overtime was not an option. We paid no rent for our cottage but, in return, I had to help milk the cows two weekends out of three and, as a kind of token payment, we got a little free milk.

In 1953, our daughter was born, and we named her Helene after her German grandmother. We were delighted with our progress and felt assured we were going the right way. The shortage of land for rotation made us decide to venture into poultry. We purchased a sectional poultry house for 120 hens, purchased 120 days-old pullets, which we reared under a Miller brooder. These pullets, code named Thornbers 101, a new hybrid strain, were bred for egg production with a low food intake. The litter was woodshavings I picked up from a local sawmill for nothing. We now had another profitable line that we could follow without additional land.

Then it was in 1957 that our son Stephen was born at Redruth Hospital, that I cut twenty-four bunches of pittisporum for the market. It took me three-quarters of an hour and the net return home was £7 10s: more than my week's wages.

I told Connie, 'If the farmer I'm working for can make a living, I can make a fortune.'

This was the time of the Suez Crisis. A local agent offered me an Austin A40 for £20, including a few petrol coupons. It was functional but it would not have won a beauty contest. Come to think of it, neither would I have done. We had great joy with our new addition – and it helped me to knock off the rough edges of my driving. In this, our last flower season with the Harveys, we tried stocks – white, red and a beautiful shade of mauve. The strain we had gave us approximately eighty per cent doubles, which was exceptionally good. This was our last season and we were hoping to find something suitable to purchase so all the available land was put into stocks.

Our flower season started really well. Our salesman, Ardindale in Sheffield, paid us half a crown per bunch, almost right through, a remarkable price for remarkably good quality stocks. In the evening, you could smell the stocks in St Erth village, some 400 yards away. The weather was fine and the Lord was good to us. I have learnt since that the Good Lord only helps those that help themselves honestly, but takes a different view on those who are caught helping themselves.

Reliable transport is a must, if you are depending on getting your goods to the station on time. A new Morris 1000 van was our choice, a good, reliable workhorse. YAF 113 was its number. It is the only car number I can ever remember.

Most of the smallholdings in the area were bought by ex-forces people who, after the war, had money to invest. They had been dreaming for years of being their own boss, self-sufficient, and especially in a beautiful area like West Cornwall.

They were fed up to their ears. But when somebody shouted, 'Jump!' they jumped.

They could not even ask, 'Why?' 'How high, Sir?' might have been permissible, for they were not best suited to self-employment.

In many cases property prices were well above their true commercial value. Many of these people had no experience and, perhaps more importantly, they lacked the self-discipline that is necessary for all self-employed people. Consequently many of them struggled and finally had to admit defeat. Their lack of success confirmed the good old local saying: 'The good life is all right, but it doesn't butter any parsnips.'

CHAPTER FIVE

Looking Back to an Earlier Germany

I believe many writers and makers of television and radio programmes often depict us Germans as silly or pompous, sometimes a great deal worse. There are, of course, exceptions to that pattern of reporting and, in May 1999, I was pleased to read a well-balanced piece of writing from the pen of Paul Johnson in the *Daily Mail*. In it he outlined some of the qualities and achievements of German people and the nation.

Here is an extract from his article:

'They are supreme in music, and for a British conductor to be asked to conduct the Berlin Philharmonic or the Bayreuth Festival Orchestra is the highest accolade.

'They are supreme in philosophy – as Professor A J Ayer used to say to me, for a British philosopher to get an honorary degree from a top German university was "no mean achievement".

'They are supreme in history, too, and when one of my works is published in German by a reputable house specialising in history, I feel I have really made it.

'They are the top nation in theology, too – and have been ever since Luther.

'Not least, from the end of the 19th century, they began to beat the British – who launched the Industrial Revolution – at our own game: producing high quality, reliable manufactured goods at competitive prices.

'Between the wars we could still outdo them, inventing in turn radar and the jet engine. But from 1949, when Germany launched its post-war economic policy, we fell, from a position of great post-war strength, more and more behind Germany as an industrial and commercial power.

'We had nothing remotely comparable to the post-war German "miracle", which made the Deutschmark the world's strongest currency.'

Now and then I am staggered by the ignorance of some people about the war and all the suffering involved on both sides.

Back in the early 1980s, I attended a man–management course at Stoneleigh – we were a mixed bunch of managers and employers – and one evening I was enjoying a quiet drink with a big dairy farmer from Dorset. During the course of our conversation – we were reminiscing over past experiences – he made an astonishing observation, saying, 'The war...you probably enjoyed it.' The memory of friends screaming in that cellar on the Dutch border for hours, while we were unable to help them, came back to me very vividly. The recollection of that fatal night can still give me nightmares fifty-five years later.

I was only fourteen when the war started and, within just a few years, was plunged into battle. Now, forty years on, I was plunged into a loss for words.

After a few moments I replied, 'You were exempt from military service because you were a farmer. You will never therefore know what fun you really missed.'

Immediately – in memory – I was back on that open ground, that October night, when bullets were raining down on us from the Americans. I remembered the devastation of our German cities. I recalled too the ignominy of surrendering – the gloom and the despair of it all.

This seemingly intelligent farmer from Dorset, a pillar of his society, school governor and serving on various committees, just had no idea about the grim realities of war – for both sides. He offered to buy the next drink but I suggested we have an early night as there were examinations the next morning.

Perhaps here I should take the verbal camera back to my beginnings in Europe. Wechterswinkel is a small village in North Bavaria – only about twenty-five houses – set in green wooded countryside. In the old days, it was very much a farming community but nowadays a number of the villagers commute to the towns where they work in factories. It's a kind of showcase village, in a protected area, but not really on the tourist map though some visitors come and have a drink and a meal in a local cafe.

The history of my place of birth goes back to about 400AD, and later on in the years 800-900AD German kaisers lived close by and the area provided a good hunting ground for the rich. Soon after the first millennium, Christianity had a great influence. It put the fear of God into the high and mighty. Kaiser and kings, *grafen* and nobility were generous with gifts of land, forests, etc. in the belief that it would ensure them similar status in the afterlife.

Recently, the church celebrated its 800th anniversary. Religion has played a large part in the area. The generosity of the nobility established a nunnery for their daughters who had not found suitors – and a generous gift came with the daughter. Farmers had to give ten per cent of their harvest to give the 'Kloster' wealth. The Reformer, Luther, found many followers in his conquest to curb the excessive power and greed of the Roman Catholic Church. In the Easter week of 1525, many nuns had already returned to the family castles, to escape the imminent threat of the atrocities of the thirty-year war. As pre-arranged, all farmers, who had not fled and felt the injustices of their ten per cent payment to the church no longer bearable, rose in rebellion. They plundered the cellars and stores of the convent, destroying all records of outstanding payments, relishing the moment. Fired by strong drink and having no respect for the holiness of the place, they set fire to the buildings, and many priceless items were wilfully destroyed.

The thirty-year war ensured the total plunder of the church buildings, and the Swedes gave the useless property to a local nobleman. The Lutherans took over administration of the area. The ringleaders of the uprising were beheaded and the followers replaced the roofs of the ruins when sober again. As in most countries, the ruling classes usually chose the best location for their own use. I can quite see why nobility chose this area, for the convent and their offspring. Perhaps I am a little prejudiced.

The after-effects of the First World War left the country in a terrible state. Inflation was rampant and came to a point when people were dealing with millions, billions, and in the end trillions, to a point when the housewife carried the money in a basket to buy a loaf of bread. Not surprising that the baker probably said, 'Keep the money but I'll have the basket instead.' Bartering was the only way to get anything. The revaluation brought some stability, but with the side-effect of mass-unemployment – an army of six million unemployed and a state with no means to provide much help for them. Many evening meals consisted of potatoes and salt. It is no wonder that many supported radical parties, who in turn created unstable governments. This was a period it is difficult to find described in German history books. Our parents remembered it. They never forgot. My family escaped the worst of that period by being self-sufficient. We grew our own corn, a mixture of wheat and rye. This was collected once a fortnight by the miller and returned a fortnight later. One hundredweight of grain brought sixty-five pounds of flour. The miller kept the rest along with resulting bran for his troubles. The flour was taken by my brother and I to the baker in the next village two miles away, in a little four-wheel handcart. A rough track qualified as a road; it was hard work. We returned with approximately half the entitlement for the sixty-five pounds of flour, which was fourteen loaves, so the other seven were collected later. Here again, the baker would retain sufficient for his efforts. No money changed hands.

Every October a pig was killed. It was usually an old grandmother sow, too big and too fat to be saleable to the butcher, that got her call-up papers. This was always an enjoyable day, for that day meat was not rationed, and we soon learned what we preferred. This ceremony was always performed by a local man from the village, who had learned his trade in his younger days. There was plenty of hot water from the big copper boiler everywhere. Soon mountains of fat were removed and melted down. Some parts had to be de-boned and cut into small cubes of sausage meat. Some of the best was mixed with bought-in beef for salami. The hams were air-dried and later smoked in the chimney chamber for use next summer. The smoking was done when only beechwood was burned in the oven. The rest was stored in oak-wood barrels and preserved in salt brine. Fruit was bottled for the winter, cabbage was sliced and again stored in oak barrels and preserved with salt and pressed to be eaten during the winter as sauerkraut. Perhaps the expression German 'krauts' originated from this preserve. Never mind: sauerkraut and a good piece of pork and dumplings provided many an enjoyable meal. Peas and lentils were dried and stored. Apples too were stored and covered with straw to guard against the frost.

It was a very different story in the big industrial centres – and only a matter of time before any political party was given a chance. So Hitler came to power in 1933 and almost overnight brought work and bread. The popular saying of the day was, as old people remember, 'He who doesn't work, can also not eat.' Not many will objectively report how things were at that time: how social improvements through help in winter and community welfare worked; how large families benefited by coupons exchanged for clothing or blankets; where workers could benefit from cheap holidays through the organisation 'Strength through enjoyment'. We pride ourselves today about our new creations. The Volkswagen was, at DM1,000, affordable for many workers.

Sport was encouraged among the youth. Roads were built. The autobahns were established in record time.

Farming was shown better ways. Better seeds were introduced. The Germans were satisfied. Factories were busy and the streets and shops full. Many elderly people will still say, 'Hitler was not all bad, not all.' Of course, this comfortable feeling changed with the outbreak of the war. Many things happened in the war that should not have happened. That part of history is well documented and to our great shame. We will not be able to forget. The press will see to that and rightly so . The terrible happenings in the concentration camps in the war years were not known to the general public. In pre-war Germany institutions for correction and rehabilitation for habitual offenders existed. In an area of two small towns and twelve villages I have only heard of one man who served time in what was locally know as a *dachau*. He had served several terms of prison and was committed; he was a drunkard and had failed to maintain himself and his family. After three months he came back, looking healthy and fit. After about eighteen months, he returned to his old ways and a refresher course of six months was the prescribed punishment. On his return, he looked well, was hard-working and God-fearing. I have not heard that he has shown any wish to return for a third time which just shows that leopards do change their spots. It only may take a little longer – and stronger medicine.

As I had entered school a year early, I could leave a year early. I overheard a conversation between my mother and the road maintenance man.

'Send Rudi to the middle school,' was his advice. This was the equivalent of the grammar school.

As my father's death was caused through war injury, the education for any dependent child was free. My mother's thoughts though were different – time I earned money. It also crossed my mind that, as places for an apprenticeship were difficult to find, she might yet succeed in pushing me towards the church. Two other boys from the village had entered the *Munster Schwarzach* – a sort of religious centre, where everybody could learn a trade and be prepared to go out into the world as missionaries or in support of missionaries.

During a school break, the manager of the firm next to the school approached our teacher, enquiring if there was anybody wishing to serve an apprenticeship with him. I was his choice – and passed the head office's personnel director's interview on 25th April 1939, only thirteen years old. First year's remuneration was DM5 per month. It was not much and was very much less than a thirteen-year-old's pocket money today.

It was a well-sought-after job with a monthly salary at the end, instead of weekly wages. One day a week, school training was compulsory. The lack of grammar-school education was a disadvantage, but I was a willing learner and after three years' apprenticeship I was the only one out of four with no further education, and the only one who passed the final test. Looking back, further education would have opened the door for me to become a manager of a small agriculture store chasing farmers half my time for bad debts; there would have been little opportunity of real progress.

Instead, I spent the first nine years of my working life in the lowest-paid industry of this country, surrounded by opportunities waiting to be explored. The short time I spent in an office taught me a little about book-keeping and the price calculations for any product. The sales price must always show the level of profit; to think of everything over purchase price as profit is to forget all other expenses.

When learning my trade I worked directly under the book-keeper, a clever fellow, but a very serious motor-bike accident had left him physically handicapped with steel plates in his head and shoulders. I always thought that he felt his job was threatened by me and his best defence was to teach me as little as possible. When the manager was called up, he took over the management job and I looked after the outside and customers' contact. (Well, I had my own back on him. When the manager returned after the war to his old job, the book-keeper had to take demotion. He wrote to me for support saying that he and I could manage the branch store and the ex-manager could probably fill the vacancy in a neighbouring larger store. But by then, I had bigger plans.)

Farm prices were government-controlled, fixed according to quality. It is surprising what the weight of one litre of grain will tell you of its quality. If you think moisture will increase the weight you are mistaken. The same price rules applied to potatoes. A small storage charge was added every month.

I was fourteen when war broke out. Social life was very limited. Dances were not permitted and a card game in the evening was about the limit. I succeeded in obtaining a Silver Sports Medal, similar to the Duke of Edinburgh Award and a Sharp Shooting Medal. My brother, two years older than me, was soon called up and I spent most of my spare time helping my mother and sister on the smallholding. Sunday was my day off. Going to the church in the morning was near-compulsory.

In the afternoon, we roamed in the woods close to the village, sometimes in company, other times just as we had done since we were five years old. No tree was too high. On my last visit to Germany, I refreshed those memories of my youth, and my mark RM was still on my favourite tree. Nobody was allowed to go near it. It was mine.

It is interesting how children and adults are drawn to woods. Maybe there is a spirit of adventure about woods. Many of them have an air of a place untrodden, an impression intensified in the autumn. Trees frequently feature in our dreams. Trees, of course, give shade and protection. So often, when I think back to growing up as a child in Germany, thoughts centre on those Sunday-afternoon rambles and I have a certain pride in knowing my initials remain on that favourite tree.

In 1942, all young men born in 1924 were all called up for the *Arbeits Dienst*. This was a service all eighteen-year-olds had to serve from the mid-1930s onwards. First of all, it was designed to lessen mass unemployment, and train everyone in the art of practical work, achieving physical fitness and discipline. After one year, they were smart, fit and not pansy boys. In wartime, these units were mostly used to follow the advancing army in Russia and keep the lines of communication in repair. As the war was going badly in Russia, the time of this service was reduced to six months, and all the young men born in 1924 were handed over to the army, without a customary home leave on changeover. Very few of those poor devils saw their home and family again. We were told that it was Hitler's orders that those born in 1925 should not be sent to the Eastern front. To lose two years of youth in the prime of their life was an unacceptable price.

I was called up to this working service in January 1943 and after some basic instructions we were transferred to Southern France, approximately fifteen miles west of Marseilles. We were supposed to serve a semi-military role. For the first two weeks, we dug out our defence along the side of the hill overlooking the bay. After that, we had to build a six-foot-high anti-tank wall from a small harbour across the beach about a mile long. With the beginning of the summer, we soon learned why our uniform was described as tropical. From seven a.m. to seven p.m. were our working hours. A pair of shorts and a pair of boots, with our feet wrapped in a piece of cotton cloth, carefully arranged, were all that was needed. Filling the mixer and laying the reinforced concrete was hard work. Sunday was a day of rest. We spent it around the sea. A favoured pastime was lying on a board half-submerged in the water asleep. After two hours, you might find yourself 100 metres from the shore.

At the end of June, we returned to base in Germany and release. I was amongst ten selected to take on a new lot of trainees and return to the South of France. At the railway stations on the way down, we saw trainloads of Italians prisoners going the other way towards Germany – they had given themselves up. Things looked bad – history repeating itself. The Italians knew more than we did. We were living in hope; they already knew that if they wanted to be on the winning side, this was the time for their traditional change of heart.

We were located in Nice on the seafront, an area previously occupied by the Italians.

Nice, here on the south-east French coast, on the edge of the Mediterranean, may be one of the great resorts of the Riviera but we all knew this was no holiday – the war was going badly and there was a good reason for our being here: to show a presence until a proper military unit took over. All the same, it was a pleasant place to be and, at a superficial level, you were not really aware of the fact that things were fast reaching such a critical stage in the conflict for Europe.

All good things come to an end. We ten were released and the new recruits transferred to the English Channel coast to build and man anti-aircraft positions. After a short holiday, I was enlisted to the airforce and transferred to South West France for basic military training for eight weeks, to be followed by transfer to a place near Brest. Our training was a continued selection of suitability for training as fighter pilots. The next hurdle was to qualify for the non-commissioned officer examination, which was a rank for fighter pilots and full qualification brought promotions.

Soon after, we were transferred to the Air Training School at Graz Talerhof in Austria. We were one of the first groups to go straight to motorised planes. Previously, all had to have had glider experience and licences. About half our group had that experience. At first, there were many lessons about navigation and aerodynamics. There were also several bombing attacks on the airfield. These attacks were more of a nuisance than anything else, causing no lasting damage. The first attack had only one hit – the quartermaster's store. The other bomb fell in adjoining woods. At the end of July 1944, following an assassination attempt on Hitler's life, there was suddenly a different air about service life. The introduction of the Hitler salute to replace the traditional military salute caused some uneasiness. The sloppy way some officers saluted indicated they did not like the change. It would have been foolish to show open defiance, which would have immediately identified the recalcitrants as possible sympathisers of the attempt on Hitler's life.

These officers were in most cases professional soldiers who had faithfully done their duty for their fatherland. They did not like the involvement in politics. A sense of urgency was noticed in our training, and anybody who had not passed his solo flying test was withdrawn. I was amongst them. In Germany, paratroops were part of the Luftwaffe, so when we were given the choice to stay in the Luftwaffe and join the second paratroop corps that was being assembled near the Dutch border at the time, we all joined. The alternative would probably have been transfer to the infantry and the Eastern front – not a popular choice. Things were not going well in the West either.

Rommel, the Commander-in-Chief, had been wounded and, with his recovery almost complete, was suddenly reported as having died from his wounds. He was a very highly regarded soldier and respected in Germany. More recent history has probably cleared up the mystery of his involvement in Hitler's assassination attempt. Had it succeeded, it is now assumed that Rommel would have made peace with the West. The jigsaw seems to fit.

The landing of the 82nd American AA landing division near Nymwegen to secure the bridge over the Rhine gave me my baptism. When reinforcements landed right in front of our noses, our luck was in. In Germany, we talked about total war. The American pilots got out and disappeared into the far distance, their gliders unguarded. As a member of a reconnoitring patrol of the 2nd Paratroop army, it was our job not to reveal our presence. The next day a light anti-aircraft gun firing four shots at a time had a rich harvest at point-blank range: our job well done.

Then came that first night of October – and the end of my soldiering war.

CHAPTER SIX

Our Future Unfolding

*T*he world from which I came offered me no advantages – only those I created.

We had been at Tredrea five years and began thinking seriously: 'We'd like a place of our own.' So Thursday evening after Thursday evening, I studied the business pages of the *West Briton*. We needed a property that had three qualities: good land where we could grow flowers, a house where we could live – and the right price. Sometimes we found what looked the right place but then discovered the price was beyond our range.

One evening I spotted a property, west of Penzance, which, on paper, seemed a possibility but when Connie enquired at the estate agents, she was told, 'It's in the wilds, miles from anywhere and there's no public transport. The nearest water supply is a stream a few hundred yards away...and there's an earth toilet.'

At least the estate agent was being honest but both he and Connie knew it was not our kind of place. Soon after though I spotted another advertisement in the *West Briton* announcing the availability of 'a house with five acres of land near the village of Praze-an-Beeble'.

I turned to Connie and said, 'If we don't ask, we shall never know.' So I made a call from the nearest phone box.

'You can come and have a look at the property at Crowan at two o'clock on Saturday afternoon,' I was told.

Where was this village of Crowan? We looked it up on the map. My only means of transport was the old bicycle, bought for £2, several years before. Anyway, I was there on time on the Saturday.

The only free-standing house was opposite the red phone box. It had a cut granite front and my heart started sinking: 'Not this for the price advertised?'

About a quarter of an hour later, the owner's wife arrived with another lady in her car. The second lady was no rival. She was interested in another property on the other side of the road. So while they looked at the second property, I was invited to inspect the field. There were sixteen horses grazing; the grass was lush and a little prod with an iron bar revealed fertile soil. A previous owner had kept lots of pigs here and all their dung was returned to fertilise the land. 'This looks promising…'

Dixcarte was a five-acre square field, sheltered from the cold north wind, facing south, with a mill stream at the bottom, the water driving a water wheel further down the village.

The house had been built about 1870 in the heydays of Cornish mining. Mining boomed and beer was popular among the thirsty miners. The Miners' Arms, as it was then called, was one of three pubs in Crowan. The village had a bigger population than today, but when the mining declined, peopled drifted away and all three pubs closed. The house was renamed Dixcarte by a teacher, a member of the well-known Bourdeaux family. There is a hotel of that name on the Channel Islands.

Legacies of the old inn were still there: the benches in the kitchen. The serving hatch in the hallway and the sitting room had been converted into one large area. Upstairs there were four bedrooms, the two biggest bedrooms were divided by a folding door which, when folded back, converted into a dance floor. There were two attic rooms, probably quarters for the servants.

The low asking price was largely due to the fact that Mr Bolitho, the gentleman selling the property, had the problem of a sitting tenant but, with his nimble mind, he suggested the elderly lady might prefer a smaller cottage. He had one such property only a short distance away – and she readily agreed.

The old inn was structurally sound, but the roof needed renewing eventually; for the time being a cement wash would keep it watertight and secure. It was central to the village, with a church right opposite. It was habitable but not modernised.

The way home is always quicker. I had the advantage too that most of it was downhill – and I was keen to tell Connie the good news – however I did not wish to appear over-enthusiastic to the Bolithos. Gordon Bolitho therefore suggested he brought Connie in his Jaguar to look around the property.

Gordon Bolitho was a genuine dealer. No city slicker, he was the kind of man who looked for a reasonable profit from a quick sale. I can still see him in my mind's eye: Gordon enjoyed good living and it showed. He was almost as wide as he was long.

Connie approved. It was September and we were expecting our second child in six weeks, but could not really move until the following May when our flower harvest would be completed. The price was £2,250. A deposit of £650 was accepted to secure the property and the rest, if and when, subject to interest payments. We had to keep it a secret from our employer for the time being – to avoid complications.

Working for the Harrys at Tredrea had been a good stepping-stones experience. Deep down, Connie and I both knew it was time to move on. The little land we had there was restrictive. The whole situation did not encourage progress. We could not grow anemones in the same ground again. Our poultry house and Dutch Light green house took away valuable growing space. Both house and land were tied to my employment – and with those facts came a sense of insecurity.

Despite all that, Tredrea was not a bad farm on which to work. Mr Harry soon became Wilfred but Mrs Harry never became Grace to any of us workmen.

We could not leave Tredrea until the following May, when our flower harvest was over. It turned out to be our most profitable but we kept our secret. Only my German friend John knew the true facts. When I eventually told Wilfred I was leaving, he took it very well. His wife did not. She was, I think, very jealous. I was becoming my own boss – with my own business and freehold. I did not know that their eldest daughter Margaret, who had been courting for some time, wanted to get married urgently. Our cottage becoming vacant solved her problem of accommodation.

Wilfred Harry lived into his eighties. He lived a comfortable life – provided he could have Saturday afternoons off to watch his beloved Magpies play football. You could get most things off Wilfred – except money: looking back – not a bad bloke, not a bad employer either.

An interesting postscript to my time at Tredrea: the farmhouse has links with a famous Cornishman who lived and worked here for a while. I often think of him when I'm in Camborne and pass Richard Trevithick's statue. There is the great Cornish inventor in swallow-tailed coat and breeches, looking up Beacon Hill. It is good that he should be remembered in Camborne because around Christmas 1801 his 'puffing devil' carried passengers to the top of Camborne Hill 'at more than walking pace'.

Trevithick, the inventor of the high-pressure steam engine and pioneer of more than a dozen engineering advances, died penniless in Dartford, Kent, where he was working on the marine engine – work which paved the way for the first crossing of the Atlantic under steam.

It is a sad story and a reminder that fame and fortune do not always go together.

A Day's Work – as the Boss

When I say the boss, please don't imagine me as a managing director, sitting in a plush office surrounded by telephones, table-top computer and a secretary. Far from it! A secretary? I would not know what to do with her. Computers I leave to the younger generation. I have only now mastered my pocket calculator.

I worked no real set hours and went on working until ten o'clock in the evening if necessary. I must have a kind of photographic mind because I never needed to go into the fields often. In my mind, I could see the picture and the progress.

Connie remembers calling me in from the field for a midday meal: 'I'd call out just one word: "Rudi!" I'd really shout out that one word and it meant "dinner's ready". If Rudi were a few minutes late, I'd keep the meal warm and moist. He said something about his meal one day and my mum said, "Liver does go hard if you're late for your meal!" '

We had no chain of command. We all worked as a team with me at the top and knew each other by our Christian names. We employed approximately twenty people permanently and up to 200 irregular daily casuals at the peak of the flower season.

There was no such thing as a typical working day in our business. First of all, farming and flower-growing are very seasonal, depending to a very large extent on the weather, for the whole season and also for any particular day. Anybody can make hay while the sun shines. To make hay while the weather is changeable demands more expertise and experience, and perhaps some luck. So to some extent, decisions have to be made under differing circumstances. I never had any difficulty making quick decisions when needed. For instance at harvest time every possible opportunity must be taken to make full use of any time the corn is dry enough in the morning to get the combine going until it gets too damp. My job would be to see that the combine harvester had been serviced, and any defective parts replaced and ready for action soon after completion of the last year's harvest. A wet weather job for the combine harvester's driver – that would be his responsibility.

Delegation is the art of successful management. We started at eight a.m. in the morning and it would be an exception if all employees would not be present at five minutes to eight. Most would just say, 'Carry on with the previous day's work?' and a nod from me would confirm it.

I might enquire, 'How much more is to be done?' He or she might volunteer that information and ask, 'What next?'

The tractor drivers would fill up their tractors, grease their implements, etc., and, weather permitting, carry on where they left off the day before.

We had no titles like manager or foreman. The only full-time charge hand was Mildred, in charge of the egg-packing of our 100,000 hen-laying unit at Tremayne. She was a very capable lady and had my complete trust. Mildred would get her information from the main egg distributors to whom we were contracted: the size, the grade, the pre-pack cartons, the quantity and the order in which they would be required. As our output averaged about 80,000 eggs a day, Mildred would sometimes know for several days ahead in which order to pack. Everything from hen to the fifteen or thirty dozen boxes was fully automated, untouched by hand. This took care of half of our permanent staff.

At about five o'clock I would normally make an appearance, showing my face and collecting the money for any eggs sold direct. There were strict instructions – no credit. Not to make it difficult for the staff, I wrote on a large piece of cardboard in large letters: 'IN GOD WE TRUST, EVERYBODY ELSE PAYS CASH.' This was displayed in a prominent place – problem solved.

Mildred also arranged the staffing, the weekend and holiday arrangements. There was normally a waiting list for vacancies. As our business grew over the years, we had no difficulty in getting suitable workers.

I was blessed with a good memory and always carried a good picture in my mind of how the progress of the crops should be. I never felt the need to inspect the fields too often. As Andrew grew more and more into the business, he knew our ways and that made life a lot easier for me. He also organised grain harvesting and drove the combine himself. Above all, he was our trouble-shooter – and he was very popular with the staff.

The daffodil flowering season was something I always looked forward to, and equally was glad when it was over. It never failed to leave me exhausted. To level the season, we started with approximately ten acres of pre-cooled 'Hollywood,' about Christmas time. These bulbs had been stored at forty-eight degrees for five weeks from early August and planted immediately afterwards. This had the effect of giving the bulbs an artificial winter and encouraged rapid growth. Five weeks' treatment gave just the right response. Less would result in later flowering and more would shorten the time before flowering, but would adversely affect the bulb production in the following year.

Our new early varieties, purchased from the experimental station, would follow in ever-increasing quantities. If the weather was cool throughout the main flowering period, the export requirements and home demand reasonably balanced the output. However, if the weather turned mild it would test everyone including me.

Flower-picking increased by 100 per cent per day and to get everything picked and marketed successfully could become a problem. If you knew the forecast before paying-out time, everybody would be asked to bring along anybody useful the next day.

They just came. We may have approached the employment exchange in the first few years but eventually even that was not necessary because the workers would ring us asking about work and we must have treated them well, because they kept coming back year after year. They would, when necessary, recommend friends and relations. So we never had any problem recruiting workers.

On perhaps half-a-dozen days in the season my day would start at six in the morning, making enquiries about prices and demand on the main markets: a quick breakfast and making a list with recorded prices and demand for the next day. By eight o'clock the two box vans are usually already full with newcomers and the drivers raring to go. I would tell the driver which field to go to and who would be in charge of them. Most pickers returned direct to the field under their own steam and Jennifer informed them where to start and what to pick.

The packers would already have started their routine and a quick visit told them which varieties were needed first. Michael would keep them well supplied from the cold store. A quick visit to the fields would confirm how many pickers had turned up direct to the field. A quick word with Jennifer confirmed in which order the picking should be done and I then returned to the packing shed where Connie left a list of prices and orders before taking her place in the packing line. It was also her job to take telephone messages and pay any pickers who left early – usually housewives with children coming home from school. The van drivers stayed in the field instructing and supervising newcomers and assisting the charge-hands. Correct picking was very important as any bunches not right would not be paid for. Generally speaking, we demanded a high standard and paid a little extra for that quality of work. We normally had little difficulty in getting our flowers picked whilst many others left fields unharvested. In the last few years, West Cornwall has looked as if it was suffering from yellow fever.

We always made our best profits from our flowers rather than bulbs. It appears that with most growers now this trend has been reversed. It's not so much the question of over-supply; this only matters at peak harvesting times, leaving room for an increase at either side, earlier and later. Being the purchaser of the largest stock from the Rosewarne experimental station of the new, earlier and better varieties has proved to be the best investment in my life. I have passed on my private collection of new breeding stock to our grandchildren. It will give them an opportunity of newer and better daffodils and perhaps see them adding to the 23,000 named varieties registered with the Royal Horticultural Society in London, choosing their own names.

Getting back to the busy day as a boss, I can see the packing shed in full swing. Michael will have kept the women fully supplied with flowers. The boxes will have been placed on a long row of tables that will be emptied one at a time as required. With a little experience, this is done so that all the bottoms of the stems will face them nice and evenly. The women pack the cardboard boxes, normally sixty bunches per box (five times twelve bunches per row), nice and neatly held in place with a spreader secured through the side of the box. The box is then placed on a line of conveyor rollers behind them, which will bring them by gravity, to be tied in twos for the home market and again placed on a pallet, stamped with the number and variety, stacked so they will hold together. I will have a list of what to send to whom and with adhesive labels addressed to the salesmen.

We normally did one variety for all salesmen to go on the first load on separate pallets, to be followed with another variety and so on, depending on how many varieties we had for that day. It was easy to count how many boxes each salesman had and Connie wrote out the invoices and stapled them onto the boxes. The total was written on an invoice for the lorry driver.

By that time the box vans should have returned from the fields to take the flowers to Marazion for delivery to a distribution centre in Eversham, to be delivered before six a.m. into the wholesale markets. Our box vans were usually loaded to capacity of approximately 200 boxes. Once these had gone we could get ready for the London market, which had to be at Marazion not later than twelve-thirty, to be followed by another load for Bristol, Cardiff, Bournemouth, Southampton and Western International, near Heathrow.

To get these vans off with a maximum load and on time was usually a rush, after which we could breathe again. At the peak of the season, the packers usually came in for two or three hours in the evening. These boxes were put back into the cold store ready for the morning. Our highest sending for one day was 1,000 boxes with sixty bunches per box for the home market and 1,000 boxes by 100 bunches per box for export. These packers had families to look after as well, but could not have done better if the business was their own. I think their husbands were very glad when the season was over. So was my wife. These packers were all good friends and the money they earned was handy but, above all, the comradeship amongst them was equally important. In the peak flower period I did not have time to read the *West Briton*, the Cornishman's bible, but I knew what was going on and my information was two or three days in advance!

Now and then of course, I had to sack someone, I remember one woman had hidden some flowers under her car.

She was fired on the spot and, within ten minutes, it was all over the place.

Another stole just half-a-dozen eggs, but if you allowed them to get away with something small like that, the next time it would be a bigger theft and the whole thing could develop into a big problem. Luckily, these were very rare cases. Generally, we had a very good team spirit.

After the last load had left it was time to pay the pickers in the field. We did not go into the field too early because that was the signal for many of them to stop work. Connie or Andrew usually helped me to pay them. Everybody came with a card signed by a supervisor, with the total number they had picked for that day. Many earned very good money. To pay 100 people went surprisingly quickly. All our staff worked as a team. Even to this day, we are still friendly with them all.

A quick word with Jennifer and the other charge-hands completed my picture of the picking. A drive around the fields in the four-wheel drive, mud flying everywhere, refreshed my mind as to the state of the crops. At the end of the day, reading the newspaper for half an hour, helped me to wind down. I have never taken my work to bed with me and, as soon as my head hit the pillow, my light went out.

At the end of the flower season, we took all the staff in the packing shed out for dinner with their husbands. The husbands were glad of the end of the season, as picking time meant it was their turn to get the meals. One ended up with the chips on the doorstep when the frying pan caught fire.

June and July were bulb-harvesting times with Jennifer again in charge in the field. We were the first to introduce bulk-handling of bulbs from the field to the grader, drying and storing, and back to the planter again in twelve-hundredweight boxes. With the large number of varieties, this was a great help and avoided getting them mixed. Bulb harvesting, selling, grading and marketing was rather more leisurely.

A writer called Napoleon Hill, who wrote a best-selling volume on the *Law of Success Philosophy*, referred to the importance of your QQS Rating. He believed in 'Quality' and 'Quantity' of Service and the 'Spirit' in which such service is rendered. It was not until long after our Dixcarte days that I heard of Mr Hill and his QQS style, but looking back, I can see that we would have obtained a very high rating – for the simple fact we worked along those very lines.

CHAPTER SEVEN

❧

Steven, our Eldest Son, Looks Back on his life, from his Cot to his Career as a Policeman

$\mathcal{M}$y earliest memory is of lying in my cot in my parents' bedroom looking up at a blue, gas-filled balloon with a gollywog on it. I was about two years old. My father was knocking it back and forth with his hand. At that time I was the youngest of two. My sister Helene would have been about five years old.

'Another early memory is when, at the tender age of about five, my sister broke the horrifying news that there was no such person as Father Christmas. I remember sitting on my parents' bed on Christmas morning looking at my toy ice-cream van in total disbelief: Father Christmas hadn't actually brought it for me!

'I can also remember one afternoon, when I was about five years old, Helene and I were playing in the sitting-room being watched over by our grandmother; mother and father were outside working. During this part of our life, we spent a lot of time with out grandmother because our parents were busy working on the farm. While we were playing, I knocked one of the ornaments off a shelf beside the fireplace. It shattered in the hearth. My grandmother was angry! But the seriousness of the moment came when as she reached the "B" in "You little bugger!" the friction between her dentures and gums was overcome by the blast of her shout, ejecting her false teeth into the hearth beside the broken ornament! So amused was I by this, that apparently I asked my grandmother if she could do it again – but I don't think she found it as amusing as Helene and I did.

'On the subject of false teeth – I can also remember it being so cold one winter that the toilet froze over, and my grandmother's false teeth froze in the jar of water.

'Growing up on a farm isn't all it's cracked up to be. Because my father was very busy building up the business I didn't see a great deal of him. He had normally already had his breakfast by the time we had ours, and quite often did not come in for tea until we were in bed.

'I also have fond memories of my grandmother taking us to the beach at St Ives. We would walk to the railway station at Praze – now no more – and catch a train, changing first at Gwinear Road and then at St Erth. I can also remember walking home along the main road picking wild strawberries in the hedgerow.

'I remember too that on a number of occasions when I was helping, the deep litter chicken houses were being cleaned out. There were areas within the chicken dung where the drinker units head leaked. These areas of dung had the same characteristics as quicksand, one foot wrong and you were up to your waist in manure! Unfortunately, being a slow learner, it took a number of occasions to identify the danger spots – a bit like my current career – if you put one foot wrong it is quite easy to find yourself deep in manure!

'It was not only due to these accidents in the chicken houses that I learnt at a young age that farming was not for me. From the age of about eight, I wanted to be a policeman: God knows why.

'I started my education at Crowan School but when I was seven I moved to Bassett Road, Camborne. It was here that I first encountered hostility because of my father's nationality, often being referred to as a Nazi, Kraut or Jerry by some of the other children, and not really understanding why. As far as I could see there was nothing wrong with the Germans – after all, my father was one. I feel that some of the teachers may have also been slightly prejudiced, but then some of them had fought in the war and even lost relatives in the conflict.

'As I progressed through my secondary education, this attitude towards me subsided. As a result of my experiences at school, I have sympathy for those people who are poorly treated purely because of their colour or race. I suppose I am fortunate in that it was only people who knew my father was German who were prejudiced. The colour of my skin, the way I dressed, did not identify me as being different.

'Some of my childhood memories are of when we took our "family holidays", which were rare, and normally meant a long journey to my father's home village in Germany. I have distant memories of my father fixing a seat into the back of our Morris 1000 van and us all setting off. I slept in the back of the van while my parents slept in a tent on the journey to and from Germany. The next recollections of Germany are when I was about six years old. We had an old Morris Oxford estate that was duly packed up and on this occasion my younger brother Andrew, who was about two, came along too. Within a few days of arriving at my grandmother's house I went down with measles and spent most of the first week in bed being reintroduced to the contents of my stomach every now and again. Not being noted for my generosity at the time, I was quite willing to share this with my brother, who experienced much of the same thing. On this visit I was introduced to the German custom of eating your pets – well, I don't think they were actually pets, but the rabbits my grandmother kept in the yard were treated like pets by Helene and myself. My sister and

I spent time picking leaves and feeding the rabbits in the cages. It wasn't until partway through our holiday we realised that the number of rabbits was declining – totally unlike what we knew about rabbits. Although I don't remember the exact cause for the disappearance, I have been told since that the rabbits we were feeding were being used to feed us! It might be just as well I didn't know at the time. Helene, on the other hand, being nine years old, became suspicious of all the meat we ate. I can also remember part of this holiday where my Uncle Albert gave me a small deer antler, which had obviously been shed by one of the deer in the woods nearby, when it matured. I still have that antler.

'I learnt that the way of life in my father's home village was different to ours. The methods of farming were totally different. They kept their animals in stalls. We would regularly go out to one of my uncle's fields on the tractor and bring in cut grass to feed the cattle. My uncle's farm comprised a number of small patches of land, dotted around the village, none of which had any hedges or fences so it was impractical to graze cattle on the land.

'As we stayed on the farm, I only really have recollections of my Uncle Albert's children – Hannelore and Hildetrude. It wasn't until our visit when I was thirteen that I met most of my other cousins. By this time some of them were old enough to be learning to speak English. Despite having a German father I could not speak German, it all goes back to the fact that he was working such long hours I rarely saw him. So I relied on their English. For the early visits, language was not a problem. We played together in the orchard and made ourselves understood by gestures and actions.

'Back in Cornwall during school-holiday times and at weekends I spent a certain amount of time working on the farm. Not having a great deal of interest in farming, I wasn't the most enthusiastic character about the work, especially when I returned to school after the holidays and heard how my friends had spent most of the holidays on the beach enjoying themselves. I suppose the main benefit of working was that I made myself a bit of extra pocket money.

'When I was about fourteen I joined the local Air Training Corp, where I learnt to shoot and qualified as a glider pilot. Really, I would have liked to have been able to fly aircraft but as I couldn't wait to leave school, I knew that I would never get the academic qualifications needed. At this age, I was keen to join the police, but always felt that I would end up having to stay at home and work on the farm, as many farmers' sons did. I was very surprised at my father's reaction when I came home with an application form to join the police cadets. I had expected him to oppose my application, but instead he advised me on filling out the form correctly.

'On 4th September 1973, I packed my bags. My mother and father drove me to Camborne Railway Station – where the train stops on Sundays – and I disappeared to Exeter where I lived for the next eighteen months. I came home most weekends. I enjoyed the cadets as there were lots of opportunities, mostly in the sporting realms, and I had not had much opportunity to indulge in sport prior to my leaving home. At the end of my cadetship, I qualified to join the Devon and Cornwall Constabulary and my first working station was Crownhill at Plymouth. Although I had spent a lot of time in Exeter as a cadet, we were quite tightly supervised at the College at Middlemoor. Arriving in Plymouth, where there were people wandering around all hours of day and night, clubs were open until two a.m., and there were places where women removed their clothing in public, came to me as quite a shock. I worked in Plymouth for four and a half years. I can't say it's a place I would have liked to spend all of my life, but it was quite an interesting time. I then spent two years at Torquay, where life was fairly hectic. My parents probably did worry a little about me and the job I was doing. I can remember the look on my mother's face when I turned up at home on a police motor cycle with my instructor; I was then undergoing a police motor cycle course. She never did like motor bikes.

'Then, at the age of twenty-five, I found myself being shipped back to Camborne. I can't say that I moved willingly as I was quite happy at Torquay at the time, but I was cheaper to move than a married man. Policing your local area is a strange experience. To wear a uniform and drive a marked police vehicle in an area where people have only previously seen you in civilian clothes feels really weird. However, during the past eighteen years, both the locals and myself have got quite used to it. During my police work, I have come across quite a few of those who I went to school with.

Fortunately, most of them are on the right side of the legal fence. I do recall an incident, however, when a stroppy prisoner was brought into Camborne Police Station and I spoke to him, addressing him by his nickname. The arresting officer asked me if I knew who he was, to which I replied, "Yeah, I used to sit beside him at school." Apparently, he had refused to give all details to my colleague and was quite upset when I recognised him.

'Now, here I am, a married man raising a son not far from where I grew up. It is only when you think back that you realise how many things have happened in between.

'On numerous occasions I have spoken to people when I have been working and when they find out my name, more often than not it turns out that they either knew my father, or have worked for him, and they seem to hold him in high esteem because of his success through hard work.'

CHAPTER EIGHT

My Motivation

Since quite an early age, certainly before I started work at thirteen years old, I was toying with the idea of emigrating one day. This probably had its roots in being ambitious and wanting to create a life better than I thought possible in our smallholding type of community.

The agricultural law of Germany was that any smallholding of ten hectares or more had to pass on to the oldest son of the family as one unit. That prevented further fragmentation of the smallholdings. There are, and were, even before the last war, some good fertile farms in Germany, especially in the north-eastern parts now yielded to Poland. In our area, all land was zero-grazed, with the cattle indoors summer and winter and all fodder had to be brought to them. The fields were on an acre or less and ten hectares in twenty patches was quite normal. In the 'twenties and 'thirties, the smallholders, being good Catholics, had large families, and when the smallholdings were passed on to the next generation, it took great courage for anybody to take over and be responsible for the parents' keep for the rest of their lives.

Looking back, it must have been a blessing that people did not live so long in those days. There was not likely to be any money to compensate the other members of the family for their loss of a share. So some were allocated one patch of land, which could not be sold to others before being offered to the smallholder first. Not much of a future then, for an ambitious young lad.

When I was released as a POW in 1948, I was twenty-three years of age, some of the best years of my young life were already gone. My decision to emigrate from Germany was slowly becoming a reality in my mind. In 1945/46 I realised how lucky I was not to be a POW in American hands in Germany: Lucky, very, very lucky. The chief allied commander circulated orders to all field commanders on 10th March 1945 – two months before the end of the war – that all disarmed enemy forces were to receive a food ration only fractionally better than the inmates of the concentration camps. Dr Goebbels warned the German people what to expect at the end of the war and this probably prolonged the war – the alternative was worse. Letters from Germany from the summer onwards about the conditions in Germany in general, and the prisoner-of-war camps there were alarming. When General Eisenhower stated that it was his intention to treat the Germans rough and tough he certainly did that. A well researched book by B Bacqut James, *Other Losses* (published by MacDonald & Co), makes grim reading. *Crimes and Mercies* – the fate of German civilians under the Allied occupation 1944-1950 by the same author – also underlines the difficult conditions. I have no intention though of getting involved in politics.

With most of our industrial machinery removed, all patents taken away, and Germany designated to become an agricultural nation, there was little hope for an ambitious young man in Germany. The future looked bleak.

In England I had two goals: to earn as much money as possible and gain maximum experience. Even in my POW time, the importance of growing anemones was probably my number one goal, to be followed by other flower crops. If I were starting all over again, it would still be outdoor flowers, probably daffodils, and some irises.

Many people keep telling me that I would not be able to start at the bottom again. When we began I was an ignoramus. I do not regard myself as an expert now, but with my current knowledge it would not take me so long next time.

A young lad had sought my advice some years ago, and he is now well on the way without having spent large amounts of money. Money-consuming hobbies must not take priority and a like-minded partner is a great help.

I think my choice to stay over here was fully justified but my ambitions could only be achieved in Cornwall and then only in the west of Cornwall. This was – and is – the best place to produce flowers. All my intentions were based on this judgement. I was always convinced my future lay in England and in West Cornwall, there was no room for compromise.

To work on a farm was for the first two years not an option, nor my first choice. My first choice would probably have been in the building industry, creating things: shorter hours, more pay. In 1951, I only knew of one farm-worker with a car, a Robin Reliant. Today every farm-worker has a car, even if it is only an old banger. But I still don't know of any farm-worker who stayed in that job all his life and made a fortune, or significantly bettered himself. Therefore, to start on your own, I regarded as the best or only option. I knew what I wanted, and the way to get there. Growing flowers for ourselves was my goal – and my enjoyment.

As Major Reeves told me when I applied for a job, 'Unless you like your job, no good work can be done.' If I had not, I would never have put in the hours and the effort. Success is a great stimulant and motivator. With the financial restraint no longer applicable, later on economy of scale made sense. So expansion not only multiplied the rewards, it reduced too the production costs per unit. My lack of a formal education no longer proved a hindrance. Had I, instead of leaving school at thirteen, had an academic education, I'm sure my life would have taken a different direction. When I was released as a prisoner-of-war at twenty-three years old, it was too late to start on an academic road. It would have taken several years to achieve a satisfactory standard and competition from a younger generation would have been severe – leaving aside the matter of finance I did not have. So, staying in Cornwall and eventually starting to grow anemones and reap the full benefit of labour, was the challenge. I believed in my own ability and I had the support of my wife. As we experienced no major setbacks in our aims, Connie left the decisions and the way we should go to me. She was never a nagging wife. She played her part in our success – and for that I'm very thankful and grateful.

CHAPTER NINE

Connie's Side of the Story

In November 1947, I joined the Woman's Land Army and came down to Cornwall. During the war years, I had been working in a factory making parts of wings for the Halifax bombers. When the war ended, I found a job in Wembley, just a bus ride from where I lived in Harlesden.

'After I had worked there for about eighteen months, a girlfriend decided to join the Land Army. I never knew what gave her the idea but on her first visit home she said, "It's a good life." After some debate, my friend and I decided we would join. However, while we were waiting for our papers, Marion changed her mind and decided to get married instead, so I came to Cornwall on my own. Little did I know, when I was dodging bombs in London, that I would travel all the way to Cornwall to meet and marry a German. That's life, I guess.

'Rudi and two other POWs were living and working on the farm that I was sent to work on. There were several other landgirls with me and we were billeted in a hostel in Penzance. It is now an industrial estate and there is no trace of the hostel.

'Rudi and I often worked together and when he had a win on the football pools he asked me out to the cinema to celebrate. After that, we started going out regularly. When I had served in the Women's Land Army for nearly three years, it was disbanded.

'When the WLA disbanded, I didn't want to go back to London, so found a job where I could live in until Rudi and I could get married. I found a job looking after two children – a boy going on five, and a little girl aged fifteen months, for a flower farmer and his wife, in a village called Relubbus. I found it very lonely after having been in a hostel full of other girls. The children were lovely and I enjoyed looking after them. I stayed there for just over a year. Rudi was working in Ruan Highlanes at the time, so we only met about halfway in Truro every Saturday afternoon, until the following spring when Rudi managed to get a job on a farm close by – about two miles from where I was living at the time.

'He took the job because there was a tied cottage that went with it. This suited us very well. Rudi had his meals with the farmer's family and slept in the cottage. He bought me a second-hand bike and in any spare time I cycled over and we started to decorate what was to become our home for nearly six years. Life was no longer so lonely, and was beginning to have a purpose. Rudi got the little plot of land ready, and the garden. All the cultivation was done by hand.

'As we wanted a church wedding, I had to return to London for three weeks before to have the banns read. None of my family had met Rudi until he came to stay a week before the wedding but they liked him, and the fact that he was a German didn't matter at all. The vicar was the only one who didn't seem so keen. He was thinking that if we had another war there would be problems. He was going to retire shortly, and we were the last couple he married. We were married at St Michael's Church in Harlesden on 17th November 1951. It actually rained on the wedding morning. My brother gave me away as my father had died when I was three years old. My cousin was best man, and everything went very well.

'My mother was brilliant at dress-making, and had made me a beautiful wedding dress. A friend with feet as big as mine – size 7 – lent me her wedding shoes, and I borrowed the veil from my sister-in-law. Someone gave me a blue garter, so I really had something borrowed and something blue. My favourite flowers were – and still are – roses, so my bouquet was of lovely little pink roses and pinks. I had a friend from my London days as bridesmaid, and my sister-in-law was matron-of-honour. I kept in touch with my friend Margaret for several years afterwards and she and her sister came to stay with us for a holiday, but as with all long-distance friendships, it faded out. Now I wonder what became of her.

'We had the reception at home, which made a lot of work for my mother. My aunts helped on the day, but she had been gradually getting things ready for the wedding feast. Things were still rationed then, but we still had quite a good party.

'After the reception, we caught the night train to Cornwall and made our way to the cottage to start our new life. I knew the cottage was quite primitive – no plumbing – but not too bad for those days. We had made it nice and cosy. We had calor gas for the cooking and downstairs lighting but we had to take an oil lamp upstairs. I am quite adaptable, so soon got used to it. We fetched our drinking water from a tap over at the farmhouse but we had a tank just outside our back door to collect rainwater for washing. It was lovely soft water, and marvellous for washing one's hair. There were steps from the yard in the back of the cottage that led up to the garden. Beside the steps was a little wall on top of which was a slab of slate – where Rudi went out to wash in the morning and after work in the evening: very invigorating, but cold in the winter. We grew anemones, muscari and even tried sweet peas one year. They weren't such a good idea. They were very delicate and didn't travel very well. A fellow workman grew some, and one day the salesman told him when he opened the boxes the blooms had all fallen off the stems. I thought that quite funny when I imagined all those bare stems.

'I will always remember the muscari. They have a rather strong perfume and at the time they were in bloom I was expecting our daughter and enduring sickness which lasted days. The smell from the flowers made it worse. It was a long time after Helene was born that I could look at a muscari without getting spots before the eyes. We also grew calendulas, which grew like weeds. We had so many at one time we had to put the jars that we put them in after bunching, in the kitchen as well. I remember during one night I dreamt I wanted to get out of bed but couldn't because the floor was full of jars of calendulas.

'Our daughter was born in October 1953, and life became busier than ever. We also had 120 laying hens and sold the eggs to a local egg-packing station. We kept the eggs in a box in the scullery until they were picked up. Those eggs had a fascination for Helene. When she was about fifteen months old, I found her one day rolling them one at a time under the gas cooker. Luckily none broke. Not like years later when we were really into poultry farming, and Andrew, our youngest son, went into the shed where we kept the eggs ready for collection. He was having a lovely time, throwing the eggs, one at a time at the wall. He was about the same age as Helene had been. I can still see him there in his rompers with egg everywhere. What a mess!

'In our last year at Tredrea, we grew stocks on nearly all of our land. We had an exceptionally good crop – white, rose and mauve, with lovely straight stems, three or four to a bunch. Our luck was in. The weather was dry and Rudi took his annual week's holiday to market them. We had a good salesman in Sheffield, and nearly all returned half a crown per bunch. Half a crown was an exceptional price in those days. It may well have been the most profitable crop we ever had. It certainly was most welcome.

'We left Tredrea and moved into a house we had bought in Crowan. The house was very solidly built, with a cut-granite front facing the road, almost opposite the parish church. Rudi went to see it first on his own, and came back to say – "You go and have a look at it and see if you like it." He was quite sure we would not find a more suitable place for our purpose at a price we could afford. When modernised, it could be perfect. My mother was living with us by then. She had retired from work and we invited her to live with us. She had been living on her own since my brother and I had left home so she accepted. She was a great help over the years. Stephen, our eldest son, was only eight months old when we left Tredrea, so she was able to mind the children while I was helping Rudi.

'When Helene was five years old, and Stephen two and a half, I went to meet my mother-in-law for the first time. We left Mum at home to look after things and set off on our journey. We went in the Morris van, which we had acquired for our business. Rudi had made a bench seat in the back for the children. Mum had made some padded covering for it and it could have the back lowered for them to sleep on. We had both only learned to drive after our first two children were born, so driving all the way to London in one day was quite an experience. Our van was classed as a goods vehicle, so our speed was restricted to thirty mph. On our way from Slough to north-west London the police traffic control kept urging us on. We were going too slow and holding up the traffic. Rudi thought he might be going to book us for parking on the highway, so we speeded up to forty-five mph and kept up with the rest of the traffic. I didn't do any driving on that journey. Like most men and husbands, Rudi preferred to drive. I didn't mind. He would have been a back-seat driver anyway. We broke our journey to Dover, staying with my cousin and his wife. We had to be up very early next morning to get to Dover in time to catch the ferry. My cousin put the alarm clock on but he got the timing wrong and we hadn't been asleep for long before

Julie came to wake us with a cup of tea. I think it was just after three in the morning. It wasn't worth going back to sleep so we got up. We hadn't been very comfortable anyway. We had the children in bed with us and Helene had a habit of flinging her arms around in her sleep.

'London was still sleeping when we drove through. It was still very early. All the traffic lights were green so we just drove straight through to Dover and found our way to the ferry in good time.

'When we boarded we were supposed to go to a deck below, but it must have been a rough crossing overnight because it seemed most people had been seasick. Instead, we stayed on the top deck in the fresh air.

'We arrived in France, and then began our journey to Rudi's home. It was quite an eventful journey. We arrived in Brussels in the evening rush hour. (Yes, they have them there as well.) In the centre of the city all roads branching everywhere, there was a little fat policeman standing on a platform in the centre, directing the traffic. The thing we found surprising, he was wearing a gun in a holster. He pointed his finger at us. We still do not know what we had done wrong – not that it matters now. We came out on the east side of Brussels and stopped for a meal. We all felt travel-weary and hot. The children were very good considering that for them it must have been an ordeal. We left the cafe feeling much better. We decided we must make the German border to find somewhere to stay the night where the language would be no problem. By the time we reached there, it was too late to find lodgings. We had a small tent with us for such emergencies, so we had to look for a piece of land on which to camp. We found what we thought was suitable and pitched the tent. The children slept in the van. We crawled into the tent, got into the sleeping bags, and fell asleep. When we woke in the morning, the sun was shining; then came the shock. We had been sleeping on land that was used for fly-tipping. A quick wash in a bowl, perched on the bonnet of the van, got the children ready and away we went. We found a lovely cafe and had a continental breakfast: hot rolls and coffee. The children had milk.

'We then travelled on to the Rhine through the south of Cologne, or Köln as it is called in Germany – I always think our way of saying it is much softer – it was a beautiful sunny morning, and the mighty river was carrying boats for pleasure and cargo. It was peace and tranquillity, and really impressive. The vineyards on both sides of the river rose steeply and everything looked good. The castles on the Rhine have to be seen to be believed. There is a feeling of history everywhere. We have been to many beautiful places in many parts of the world, but the part of the Rhine between Cologne and Rudesheim has to be among the best. We followed the Rhine southwards and when we wanted to stop for lunch we found a typical German Biergarten, and sat in the shade of a chestnut tree. The weather was so hot it was pleasant to eat outside and listen to the sound of the flowing river. This was our first real holiday since we were married so we were quite pleased with ourselves. We had managed to take a break at long last.

'We couldn't stay too long to admire the scenery as we intended to reach Wechterswinkel that night, and we still had a long way to go. After we left the Rhine, we speeded up our journey on the autobahn. That was an experience.

'Everything moved so fast. Arriving at our destination quite late, if I can recollect correctly, my mother-in-law (she will be referred to as Oma, which is German for grandmother) was already in bed. Rudi's brother Albert and his wife were just about to retire when we arrived. Rudi hadn't told them we were arriving by van, and someone had been to the station to meet every train. Mean wasn't he? When we weren't on the last train, they thought we weren't coming until the next day. Rudi wanted to surprise them, and he did. After all the greetings were over, we were shown our bedroom. The bed was big enough for us and the children. I think it was the width of two double beds, and, of course, the enormous duvet.

'Next day the children and I were introduced to the family. Rudi had to do all the translation as I could not speak a word of German. Rudi did try teaching me one winter. I was expecting Andrew at the time and I used to fall asleep so he gave up. Albert had two daughters about the same age as Helene and Stephen. The children all got on very well in spite of them speaking different languages. They seemed to understand each other without speaking. They even managed their falling-out sessions as well.

'It was haymaking time and several of the afternoons we all went into the fields and Rudi helped with turning the hay. Hedwig, Albert's wife, had arthritis in her hips but she still did her share. Oma was out there as well. It was a real family affair. Oma must have been in her sixties, but she still worked hard. Like most of her generation, she had her hair drawn back into a bun at the back. She was the one who ruled the roost.

'Rudi took us to all the sightseeing places that he had known when he lived there. There were forests all around the village and when it was so hot it was lovely to walk there in the shade. It was so hot that I even enjoyed drinking cold black coffee – very refreshing.

'His two sisters were within visiting distance and we were invited over for a meal with each one. Emma lived on a farm near the East German border. It was well guarded, not to keep people out but to keep them in. Hildegard lived on a farm belonging to her mother-in-law, but her husband was a heating engineer. There is a beautiful lake surrounded by hills and the forest near Rudi's home, and one evening while we were there they had a lovely firework display. It was just getting dusk and at the finale they had some coloured rockets which lit up the whole area. I will never forget it.

'Our stay with the family ended after a fortnight and it was time to make our way home. We wanted to visit some places of interest on the way back. The children had been very good, although in the mornings on the long journey they would squabble in the back of the van from the moment we started the journey. But around ten o'clock they would both fall asleep and we had peace for the rest of the morning.

'Our journey over, after a week, we made our way to the ferry. We arrived in Dover quite late and headed for my brother's house. He and his family lived in Harlow, Essex at that time and we broke our journey overnight, staying with them. We drove through London's West End around midnight. It was still very busy. We arrived in Harlow around two a.m. and, even though they had gone to bed, we were made very welcome.

'Next day it was back to Dixcarte and work. Over the next few years our land and business grew. We had been working on our own up until then but we needed some help so we employed a woman who was a neighbour. Elinor was her name and she lived in a cottage in the village with her mother. She had two sisters who were married but she always remained a spinster. She wasn't very bright but was a good worker. Later on we employed an Italian through an agency.

We weren't very well known locally and it was difficult to get staff. Rocco was a typical southern Italian – quite short and very dark-skinned. He could speak no English but soon picked it up. He had come to England to meet his bride, then living with her brother in Nottingham.

Rocco had never met her. It was an arranged marriage. He had brought a suitcase full of Italian sausage and salami. We had a spare room downstairs for him and we could smell the spicy smell after he had been with us for a few days. He had hung all the salami and sausage along the curtain pole near the window. It smelt like a delicatessen. Well, he couldn't keep it in the suitcase. It would have deteriorated, so we didn't object. It wasn't too bad as long as he kept the door shut. We managed to get him on a train to Nottingham, after a few weeks, to meet Julia, his bride. We gave him a note for the guard on the train, telling him where to put Rocco off. After a few weeks of getting things organised for him, he went to Nottingham for his wedding. He had settled in with us, and Julia was coming back to live with him and work for us as well. When Rocco first came we were growing violets and it was his job to pick them. After a few days, it started to rain, not very hard, but he was quite sure he shouldn't work when it rained. An Italian who had married a Cornish farmer's daughter lived quite near, so we took Rocco over to see him to sort out a few things. He was told if he didn't work in the rain he would hardly work at all. It rains quite a lot in Cornwall – you just had to put on your mac and wellies and get on with it.

'While Rocco and Julia were with us, our youngest son Andrew was born. My mother was a great help during that time. When Andrew was three months old I was out helping Rudi again and Mum looked after Andrew. Helene was seven years old and at school. Stephen was four and a half so he would soon be old enough to go to school. Rocco stayed with us for almost a year. He wanted to go to Nottingham where Julia's relations lived so we let him go before his contract expired – there were no hard feelings.

'There were a few other children living in the village and I used to take them all to school in the van. We started to buy more land and our flower business really flourished. We managed to employ more staff. We grew alstromeria, chincherinchees, and anemones for a while before we concentrated on daffodils. We had also started poultry farming in a big way. We started with what was called deep litter. There were wooden nest boxes around a wire-covered pit for poultry droppings, and the floor surrounding them was filled with wood shavings. We started off with one house holding 1,000 laying hens brought on from day-old chicks. Over the next three years, we built a house a year to hold 3,000 birds each. We employed a boy to look after them. He lived with us as he came from a missionary family. He had been to college and wanted some experience in poultry farming. He stayed with us for about a year before moving on. We changed over to the cage system later on. The first cage unit we had was a hatch house for 10,000 birds.

'As the children grew older they helped to pick up the eggs. Helene wasn't very keen on hens but as they were in cages she didn't mind so much. She really had a phobia about birds.

'I took them to London for a holiday one year and went to Trafalgar Square. Helene didn't like the pigeons but was quite happy feeding them until one perched on her head. That finished visiting Trafalgar Square. The children always loved animals and Helene would always be asking, "Why can't we have a dog?" She was told that we couldn't afford one. The people next door had a little corgi and one day Helene said, "The Williamses must be rich." I asked her why and she said, "Because they have a dog." Eventually we bought a golden retriever puppy – Sally was her name. The children adored her. She used to go everywhere with us. Until we really got involved with daffodils, I used to take the children out on a Tuesday. That was my day off. Sally came too. Sadly, she only lived to be nine years old. Mum missed her because she used to take her for walks. Mum was always a good walker, which was probably why she lived to be eighty-nine.

'The children were growing up now and, at eleven years old, Helene started going to a riding stables on a Saturday morning. She had passed her 11-plus examination, and went to Camborne Grammar School where some of her friends went riding. She earned her money to pay for it picking violets and Rudi let her have whatever they sold in the market. When she was fifteen, Rudi managed to find the money to buy her a horse. We had a little shed in one of our fields, which he converted into a stable. Unfortunately, the horse turned out to be really unsuitable. The previous owner wouldn't take him back, so we did a swap for a lovely gentle mare from another riding school. That turned out to be another disaster. She went lame after a few months and the vet told us she had a condition called "ringbone". She was unsuitable for riding again. The vet also told us that she was older than we were led to believe. In the end, she went to an old horses' home. That put Rudi right off horses! By the time Helene was sixteen she started going to a riding school in Penzance. Stephen decided he would like to go as well. He was thirteen. Then Andrew followed, he was eight.

'After they had been going for a few weeks I decided I was going to do something I had always wanted to do as well – horse-riding. I was forty-four at the time and Shirley's husband, Theo, said I had more guts than brains! Rudi didn't say anything but he wasn't very keen. He had the mistaken idea that after my first lesson I would give up. Instead I came home full of enthusiasm and said I was going again next week. Helene went away to college at seventeen so it was just the boys and me. We still had Sally then, and Mum used to come with us and I would drop her off with Sally at Penzance promenade to go for a walk. Rudi never came, preferring to be doing something around the farm. I went to that riding school for five years. I really wanted a horse of my own but Rudi said to own a horse you had to be a lady of leisure. There was no arguing about that, but I had some help from Helene when she left college. She came home and found work in an office in Helston. By this time we had a big workforce and one of the women bunchers knew of a horse for sale. She said, "Why not try and see how you get on with him?" It was Grand National Day when we went to see him.

'He was no streamlined thoroughbred, but we liked him. Helene rode him home and he was put into a field sharing it with a neighbouring farmer's cattle. I bought him with the money I had saved from flower packing. When we employed more staff Rudi paid me a wage, the same as the other women. I put the first £50 I earned in premium bonds and the first draw it was in after six months I won £50. That went back into another bond. I had three wins altogether. I paid £350 for the horse and still had £135 left in bonds. I've since had a couple of small winnings.

'We called the horse Sirius. That was my brainy daughter's suggestion. We took the name from a map of the stars. He was about ten years old and became a family horse – except for Rudi that is. I often tried to get Rudi interested, told him he didn't know what he was missing. Helene eventually found work in Exeter and left home but the boys used to ride, especially Stephen. Stephen took Sirius to a local horse show one Sunday. He took him into the Family Horse class and the judge said, "Isn't he a bit big for a family horse?" So Stephen remarked, "You haven't seen our family." He even went hunting a few times. Sirius loved the excitement and there was no holding him back.

'I made friends with a woman who owned a few horses and we used to go out riding together. Andrew borrowed one of her horses and we three used to ride together. I visited parts of the countryside that I had never seen before. Stephen, by this time, had joined the police force as a cadet, so he was away from home. I had Sirius for fifteen years before he sadly died. He was quite a character, with a mind of his own. We had many a battle over who was going to be boss, but riding gave me a wonderful sense of freedom. I always remember riding on my own on misty mornings when there was just the two of us. Everything would be quiet and we were alone. It was only after arthritis in my hips overtook me that I had to give up riding.

'The children were all grown up by now. Helene was married and expecting our first grandchild when my mother died. She would have loved to have seen the baby, but she died in January, shortly after my sixtieth birthday. Charlotte was born in March. By now, it was only in the very busy daffodil time that I was needed. Instead, I took over the role later of helping with the grandchildren. Helene and her family live in the farmhouse that Rudi had bought with the land, and Stephen and his wife have a bungalow in Crowan. Helene had a lovely boy two years after Charlotte was born. His name is Alexander, and Stephen and Hilary have a boy called Daniel.

'When Andrew was old enough to look after things at home Rudi and I started on our "twice a year" holidays. We began with a cruise. It should have been on the *Canberra* but this was at the time of the Falklands War and the day I collected our tickets from the travel agency *Canberra* was requisitioned for the navy. We managed to get another cruise doing the same places on a Russian cruise ship. I still feel cheated! Over the next few years we went to America twice, Canada on a farm tour with Dalgety, China with the same company, a five-week tour of South America with Saga, Greece, Turkey, Egypt (where we spent our fortieth wedding anniversary) and we had a very pleasant surprise when we were presented with a large bottle of wine, a beautiful bouquet of roses for me. We sat on a special table with some friends. It was also a birthday of another passenger. The entertainment was provided by the shipping company – an Egyptian belly dancer. We had a special cake and the birthday girl also had birthday cake. We were travelling home next day and I managed to get the bouquet back to Cornwall in one piece. I couldn't have left it behind.'

CHAPTER TEN

Business Philosophy

*A*n American called Dr David Schwartz has written a book entitled *The Magic of Thinking Big*. That book has sold over 2,000,000 copies and I am not surprised because most people want a higher income, financial security, a worthwhile job, power and influence and greater enjoyment in living.

Well, I'm not planning to write a book on this big subject but I'm devoting this chapter to my business philosophy – and though it mainly relates to our enterprise here in Cornwall I feel it will be of interest and value to many who are starting their own business – or have travelled a little way down that road.

The desire to work for ourselves is with many of us, but often for the wrong reasons. If you are your own boss, you have a very hard taskmaster indeed. He demands a strong sense of duty to your intended goal. After all, you must research thoroughly if there is a demand for what you intend to provide, be it a service, a product, or just knowledge that you have and others might want.

If you want to produce or grow something – as it was in our case – the first question to ask is this: 'Is there a genuine demand for our product?' The answer must be 'yes'; otherwise there is no point or profit in the operation.

The next question is simply one word: 'Where?' Your product or products must go to major areas of population. There is nothing to be gained by sending to the remote Highlands of Scotland or any other thinly populated region.

Question Three: 'How do we get our product there?' You need reliable transport for your product to be in market by four to six a.m. Late arrival can cut your price by half.

Reliability is more important than a penny or two cheaper in transport costs. Visit your markets occasionally at four o'clock in the morning. See your produce arrive. Is your packaging strong enough to stand the transport? Talk to your agent. How does he compare with others? Speak to the buyers. Have they got any suggestions to make? Compare your product with others. Are you satisfied that this way is the best way to market your produce? Supply-and-demand is the major market force. Quality and scarcity produce bonuses. Avoid overloading the market. Diversity to many markets can at times double your net profit.

Always present your product to the best advantage. If a prospective buyer is not impressed with the appearance of your goods he is not likely to buy from you. Do not try to hide the odd inferior article. Remember, the buyer will have found it before his next purchase the following day and this is not something you want to be remembered for.

You want to establish a reputation as a supplier of quality goods. Your agent can look and match your goods with a client's order, often agreeing the price at the end of the market. Always remember a good reputation is built over a long period, but it can be lost overnight.

With the continued expansion of our flower-growing business we realised that the marketing of our flowers through commission agents would soon become out of date, and we progressively diverted more to the export market through our membership of Lingarden, a marketing company we had originally known as Selected Growers Limited. Their rules were strict but fair, and all flowers were harvested before showing any colour and marketed and distributed throughout the continent. Quality, uniformity, and good presentation were an absolute requirement. Quantity was not a problem and nearly all were sold in advance. Sometimes we knew the price several days beforehand and were invited to take part for a specific order. Economy of scale had started to play an important part by now. The bulb business increased, but flowers were the most profitable.

Where is the best place to produce whatever you thought most appropriate to fulfil your dream?

The climatic advantage of West Cornwall is, in my opinion, the best suited to growing daffodils in the world. Our damp, mild and moist climate, not entirely frost-free and with an approximately five degrees lower summer temperature than the rest of the country makes it ideal for daffodils. It is better than even Jersey or Guernsey. Our flowers are of better quality and produce longer stems, which is very desirable, and we are approximately two weeks earlier. Lincolnshire has a much harsher climate and again is much later than here. Their produce is inferior. Lincolnshire is not acceptable for export of bulbs to the USA, because land free from potato eel-worm is essential and must carry a certificate from the Ministry of Agriculture. Therefore, our bulbs carry a premium in the marketplace because they always could be exported at a higher price to the USA.

There is a good demand for early yellow trumpet daffodils in the USA as Washington and Oregon only start producing at approximately the end of January. The distance from the west coast of the USA to the marketplace on the east coast is comparable in distance and cost-wise. Prices obtainable are generally considerably higher than over here, or on the continent.

As for the Scilly Isles, they are no longer any serious competition because of uncertain transport difficulties; the

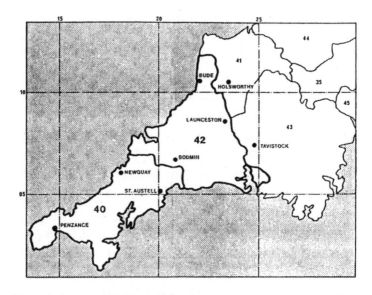

Area 40 is south-western Cornwall, with dairy and livestock farms and some horticulture.

40 (Truro Division) is comprised of Districts 778, 779, 780, 781, 782 and parts of 775, 776.

Area 42 is north-eastern Cornwall, a livestock area with some mixed cropping.

42 (Truro Division) is comprised of Districts 771, 772, 773, 774, 777 and parts of 711, 775, 776.

Cornish climate

AREA 40
Latitude 50·2°N

Average Height 83 m (272 ft)
Height Range 0–200 m

Month	Temperature Air °C	30 cm Earth °C	Rain mm (in)	PT mm (in)	κ coeff	Sun hrs/day	Day length hrs	Rad. mw-hr per cm²	Ill. kilolux -hrs
JAN	6·0	5·9	113 (4·45)	5 (0·2)	—	1·9	9·8	75	85
FEB	5·9	5·8	79 (3·1)	13 (0·5)	—	2·8	11·2	130	155
MAR	7·4	7·0	78 (3·05)	33 (1·3)	—	4·3	13·0	240	290
APR	9·1	9·8	60 (2·35)	58 (2·3)	5·1 (0·20)	6·2	14·9	365	445
MAY	11·4	12·5	72 (2·85)	84 (3·3)	7·1 (0·28)	7·2	16·8	470	570
JUN	14·1	15·2	57 (2·25)	93 (3·65)	7·9 (0·31)	7·4	17·9	525	645
JUL	15·7	16·7	73 (2·85)	91 (3·6)	7·4 (0·29)	6·8	17·4	470	615
AUG	15·6	16·6	87 (3·45)	76 (3·0)	7·1 (0·28)	6·3	15·7	395	490
SEP	14·4	15·4	88 (3·45)	48 (1·9)	6·1 (0·24)	5·0	13·7	295	375
OCT	12·1	12·8	100 (3·95)	22 (0·85)	—	3·7	11·8	185	230
NOV	8·8	9·4	118 (4·65)	8 (0·3)	—	2·4	10·3	100	120
DEC	7·2	7·2	122 (4·8)	4 (0·15)	—	1·8	9·4	65	75
Total	—	—	1047 (41·2)	535 (21·05)	—	—	—	—	—

Growing Season: 322 days Feb 20 – Jan 8
Potential Transpiration: 519 mm (20·45 in)   Effective Transpiration: 459 mm (18·05 in)
Grazing Season: 275 days Mar 4 – Dec 5   Grass Drought Factor: 13 days
Degree – days above 10°C May to Oct: 765
Winter degree – days below 0°C: 5

Mean last frost: Early April

	Median	Quartile Range
Maximum Summer SMD	89 mm	62–100 mm
Return to Capacity	Oct 5	Sep 12 – Nov 7
Excess Winter Rain	500 mm (19·8 in)	395–640 mm
End of Capacity	Apr 27	Apr 4 – May 21

Irrigation Need	Frequency (Years in 20)	Adjusted Need Mean	Max
Plan 3	15	75	115
Plan 4	10	65	85 mm

possibility of large-scale production does not exist. Our new Rosewarne breed, of better and earlier daffodils, has put the nail in their coffin. They are now mainly only producing Sol d'ors. Even Holland, the traditional home of the bulb industry, has great difficulty in competing with us for their 'greenhouse forcing' crops. Our bulbs are less fleshy and healthier and can be planted in greater numbers per square metre and flower a week earlier than those grown in Holland and therefore give the Dutch grower a greater return per square metre.

We have always invested in the best varieties available and this is probably the greatest single factor in our success. A director of the biggest local competitor stated at the Spring Flower Show in Spalding that when they bought a lorry-load of bulbs in 1990 for £200,000 from Rudi Mock they thought it was madness. 'We now know we bought gold.' This was the best advertisement I could have wished for in our forthcoming sale.

We made many good, genuine friends in the locality. I must admit there were also a few whose envy was very evident. I recall a public meeting where one of our less successful competitors went to great lengths to draw attention to the fact that he was a son of a well-established Cornish farming family whereas I was, 'a jumped up so-and-so from God knows where'. It was followed by a long silence, with me searching desperately for an appropriate reply. I could only say, 'Whatever your ambitions in life, I am no threat to them.' This little episode caused a good laugh on many later occasions.

My advice to any future entrepreneur is when an opportunity is recognised for its potential, think about it carefully. Does it fit in with your plans for the future? Will it require additional resources and will these be available if required? Don't draw attention to the fact that you are interested. If your decision is made in favour, do not waste time. If a tender is required, never quote a nice round sum. Others might think of that figure. What it is worth to you is what matters – so offer just a few pounds extra. I once made an offer for a choice building plot thinking it to be worth about £5,000 at the time. My offer of £5,025 was accepted.

Later I was approached by the under-bidder wanting to purchase part of my newly acquired land, but only about five per cent and of no use at all to me. I learned that his original offer was £3,000 to be increased to £4,000 and final offer of £5,000 was made, believing that he was bidding against himself. Had I offered £5,000 as well it would have gone to him, as he was the first to offer that price. There is a lesson is to be learned. If it is worth £5,000 it is worth £5,025. I felt sorry for the dear old fellow so I sold him the five per cent he wanted most for £3,000. I was left with probably the most desirable building plot in the area. Don't be too harsh with your judgement on me. His £3,000 investment was later sold as part of a new development with an asking price of £180,000. Without that purchase, there would have been no access and no sale. The best deals in life are those where both parties are happy and satisfied.

In life – and in business in particular – circumstance change. They change to such a degree that, before embarking upon a business project, one needs to ask – and answer – certain important questions. What works today might not work next year. What is acceptable for one generation may be unacceptable for another.

What might have been a good idea and profitable when a son takes over from his father, may no longer be the case twenty years later. The dairy industry is a good example. It had been the backbone of farming in this area for many years. Fifty years ago many farmers around here milked no more than twenty cows, employed one workman, and made a good living. Today forty cows and no workmen make a farmer feel very insecure. Approximately forty per cent of all the milk produced in this country comes from the south-west, yet consumption in the area is at a guess only five per cent of the total production. So thirty-five per cent of the nation's need will have to be transported to perhaps 250 miles away each day. While the milk quota gave, and still is giving, some protection for the time being, what is going to happen after the year 2006? Will our good growing conditions in the south-west be enough to compensate for the extra transport costs? Will the economy of scale close to the place of consumption be decisive? Would imports from the continent be a problem? The distance from there to our major towns is comparable. Should the smaller dairy farmers sell their quota now while it still has a value? I am thankful that I was never drawn into the dairy farming business. The seven-day week and early rising did not appeal to me. The prohibitive start-up costs put it out of the question, even if I had wanted to. To me there is only one thing worse than being tied to a cow's tail for seven days a week: that is having a noose around your neck.

That raises another question I have never found an answer to: why has Cornwall, being so suitable for daffodil flower and bulb production, never taken advantage of this great gift? The majority of this highly profitable industry is taken advantage of by people coming from outside the county, and with remarkable success. The government had set up the Rosewarne Experimental Station and breeding better, healthier daffodil varieties was probably its greatest success. The opportunity for the local growers was there, but it was never fully taken advantage of. I do not intend to embarrass some members of the Cornish Area Bulb Growers Association. When we had a meeting to make an offer for the stock of 150 parcels of selected and tested very-high-quality foundation stock of bulbs, for most it was the biggest opportunity missed. For me, it was the best opportunity taken, and the inclusion of this stock in our retirement sale guaranteed its success.

One other very important item in where to start any enterprise is the availability of suitable labour. Here in West Cornwall the closure or reduction of many old established firms like Holmans of Camborne, made it an area with a very high rate of unemployment. We had no difficulty in establishing a good reliable labour force. Much of our work was seasonal, involving long hours – seven days a week were unavoidable. I look back with great satisfaction at the team spirit and understanding we got from our employees. It was always appreciated. Jobs had to be done, like all flowers picked in the day had to be brought in and put in the cold store, had to have the field temperature taken out of them to arrest the opening process, had to be packed and despatched for various markets the next day. If the man delegated for this job felt he could not complete before darkness, for one reason or another, he would ask someone else to take a van or tractor out to help. There was no need for me to get involved. It was at the workmen's discretion if overtime was required to complete a job and I never questioned any overtime sheets on Friday. Our main tractor driver was also a trained agricultural machinery mechanic. He was a great asset to us with any day-to-day breakdowns. Arthur would always see to such matters and sometimes, with some help from another ex-agricultural machinery mechanic, in the evenings or weekends.

We never had a tractor or other vehicle in a garage for repair. Repairs and spare parts are today one of the major outgoings on farms and most are quite capable of doing their own welding and many repairs, not by choice, but out of necessity. We were fortunate in that our youngest son Andrew chose to stay at home with us. He was exceptionally practical with machinery and learned quickly from others. He was soon equal in most jobs. Most of our electrical repairs were also done by a local self-taught man with a wide knowledge ranging from milking-machine installations to almost anything you can think of, to the most complicated control-box automation in the poultry houses – and the fully automatic egg-packer widened his field of knowledge. He did not disappoint us. Andrew was also very keen on electronic gadgetry, and he and Peter were good mates. One other good point about Andrew and Peter was that, whatever the time, they would not leave the job until that piece of machinery was working again. All these things made a vital contribution to our continuing progress. One mistake, which many people starting up in business make, is employing too many unproductive people like managers, a secretary and a foreman. We never made that error. As our start was from the very bottom, the question never arose. Even when we had twenty permanent employees, I could not see justification for such overheads. In the egg-packing station we had a woman in charge of the day-to-day operation, who was only responsible to me. She was, as you might say, 'hands on', delegating who should do what, ensuring efficient running and helping when and where it was needed. I had neither the time nor the inclination to interfere – nor a reason to do so. I might call in for a few minutes a day or might not. She had no title. She arranged her own staff, kept all necessary records and accounted for all throughout. Mildred had the respect of the girls working under her and I trusted her completely with cash sales. You could not wish for anybody more suited for the job. Mildred was with us and running our poultry enterprise at Tremayne from the very beginning right up to the sale to Horizon Poultry farms. She left soon after.

With Andrew coming on, life became easier for me. I always looked forward to the beginning of the daffodil flowering season. It was, after all, our single biggest source of income. It started with approximately ten acres of precooled Hollywood, just before Christmas, followed by early, mostly new varieties from the ex-Rosewarne, which progressively played an increasing importance in our flower production. The main season came normally at the end of January/early February, depending on the weather and temperature in the autumn. This is normally four weeks where my involvement would reach its limit and mine, making sure we have the right amount of pickers for the next day when the last lot is loaded into refrigerated lorries. Andrew and I usually went out to pay the pickers. In the earlier days, Connie would also take one lot, usually in separate fields. We did not normally go out before four o'clock because when the vans appeared in the fields it was usually a signal to stop for most of them. This made sure they had done a full day's picking. The supervisors recorded the numbers of bunches picked on their cards, multiplied it by the price per bunch, paid in cash, and said, 'See you tomorrow.' My faithful companion, a German Shepherd named Heidi, looked over my shoulder to watch proceedings. Quite large sums of cash were paid out this way I recall two weeks running, we paid out £28,000 per week – a lot of money in those days. Cash was usually collected in two or three lots per week – the larger amounts by me, but often considerable amounts by Connie. It may not have been wise to collect such amounts without a guard fifteen years ago. Today it is almost unthinkable.

Our working day started at eight a.m., and the staff was always there well on time. My day started a little earlier, with an enquiry about the market trends in the main markets. At seven-fifty-five a.m. I ensured the permanent staff had already allocated the transport for any newcomers and we quickly decided where to go and what to pick. Most pickers had already gone straight to the field and the supervisors with whom they had been working with the day before. This gave us a good advantage over another large-scale grower where all had to assemble in the yard and were very often sent back the way they came from, as well as having to move to different sites during the day, mostly with their own transport. In the evenings, they also had to return to the yard again to be paid – as a result a lot of time was wasted. Our arrangement enabled our pickers to spend the maximum time picking and some very good money was earned by many of them. Others preferred a more leisurely approach – to take a rest now and again. There were also many housewives, with school-age children who preferred nine to three and Saturday and Sunday when their husbands were home and could look after the children. While we had flowers to pick, anybody was welcome, any time between eight and five, as long as the bunches were of the required high standard.

Time did not matter. We even had some of the new-age travellers at times. They were probably the least reliable. Their standard of work was often good, but their needs and availability for work did not match – or clashed with the day when the DHSS was payable. The picking was organised by the supervisors, which left me free to spend most of the time in the packing shed and the marketing side. Connie took most of the phone calls and prices from the salesmen, and passed them on. Any consignment to the northern markets like Gateshead, Hull, Middlesborough, Sheffield and Bradford, had to be at the depot by ten-thirty a.m. This was always a hectic time getting them on the van and away on time. Every salesman's lot was always on a pallet or pallets and checked as loaded. Next came the Midlands by one p.m. There was a list from me, with what for whom, which was always subject to last-minute alterations due to phone calls from salesmen. Covent Garden was by three p.m., Bristol, Cardiff and Southampton were last. If there were exports for that day they would have to be gone by six p.m. and would go direct from our cold store into the refrigerated lorries. By four p.m. it was paying-out time. Connie usually had the money-boxes prepared with plenty of small change in their compartments and spare change in little bags for refills. When we started first we paid an hourly rate, according to age, for schoolchildren. That was a daft thing to do. After the first week we realised many became older by the day. Of course they did, but not by that much! It took a long time for me to live it down, when two brothers came for payment together. The smaller one insisted he was two years older than his much bigger brother! You can imagine my embarrassment when the next day he brought his birth certificate to prove me wrong. It was a pleasure to see the fourteen-year-olds' delight at receiving their first hard-earned pay. You could almost tell their age by the change in the expression of their faces. And I noticed the girls kept their smiles much longer.

This way of payment was highly unsatisfactory. The changeover to payment per bunch improved things. If we were not quite sure that one supervisor was strict enough with somebody, that person would be told that Jen, our number-one supervisor, was a little short of numbers and to report to her the next morning. The terms of employment had to be strictly irregular – daily, casual flower-pickers for payment in cash daily, with no commitment to further employment by either party. This was a special agreement between the Farmers' Union and DHSS about not having to take out Income Tax and National Insurance contributions at the end of each day, which would have been impractical and killed both the flower-picking and the industry stone-dead. Names and addresses and the total earnings of the individuals had to be prepared and reported to the local tax office at the end of the year.

Pickers knew themselves that if the field was not finished, there would be work there again or in another field. If the weather forecast indicated wind from the south-west we knew very well that the next day there would be more flowers than today. Pickers would be asked if they had any friends or knew of anyone wanting to pick and to bring them along. We always had our flowers picked while many others had fields-full left. I usually had a chat with the supervisors about the next day: how long it would take? What comes next? A quick trip with the four-wheel drive confirmed the picture for the next day and the state of other varieties to follow. At six o'clock or soon after, we had our evening meal, and everything was in a lower gear. The weather forecast usually gave an indication whether my expectations for the next day were likely to be correct. However, should south-westerly winds and mild weather be forecast, our expectations next morning would be trebled.

You could see the flower stems showing approximately two inches of pale yellow at the bottom. That is how much they would have grown overnight. Anybody enquiring about flower-picking in the last four weeks would get a call and be asked to bring along anyone they could think of. The family was all glad when the flower season was over and the telephone stopped ringing. In the packing shed, local schoolboys would make up flower boxes for the next day on electrical staple machines. At peak times, the packers would also come in during the evenings. They all had families to look after but they were very helpful – and a good bunch of people. They were probably happier with the daffodil season than their husbands were. With the progressive decline in the wholesale markets and increasing demand for export, some varieties had to be abandoned. The exporters will only take the traditional yellow trumpet daffodils and will not accept the many attractive bi-colours. Golden Ducket, a good yellow double, is also acceptable. It is quite possible for flowers that had been in the cold store for at least twelve hours to be packed for the next day and kept cool in boxes in cold store.

While the rush of daffodil season was on, I quite happily worked all hours for seven days a week without feeling any ill-effects. I always felt that the body is like an engine, where the governor adjusts the output to the demand of the engine. When that demand is met or reduced, it decreases the output accordingly. For the first fortnight after the rush was over, I always felt exhausted. I suppose nature has its own way to deal with life as it is.

While flowers were our most profitable line, bulbs were regarded as a quite profitable bi-product. Here life had a more normal pace. With our policy of always increasing with the better and more expensive varieties, this was also reflected in the sale price. Here we were under a contracted obligation to sell all our output to Lingarden. While my knowledge about daffodils was all gained from others, I feel the introduction of the bulk-handling of bulbs in approximately half-ton boxes was my contribution to the industry. It had been tried by many in Lincolnshire with a slatted type of box as used for potatoes, and failed. So our idea was new and readily taken up by the Experimental Station at Rosewarne – and recommended by them. It is especially useful to avoid getting varieties mixed up. All our handling is based around this box and the ventilation is controllable. The drive-in sterilising tanks, the hot and cold storage, grading system etc., even the trailer to bring in the bulbs from the fields and return them for planting again, and the loading of the planter is done in these boxes. This system has stood the test of time. The bulbs are picked up in these boxes in the fields, saving time and effort. I take great satisfaction that our handling system has proved so successful. The sterilising was done in our drive-in tanks. Four boxes, two tons per tank, eight tons at a time. One hour soaking. Three hours at 116 degrees with half a per cent of formaldehyde and wetting agent in the water, followed by a quick fan-drying. Our planting was well organised and the boxes were emptied into the planter with a tipper attached to a tractor.

Bulb-growing land should have a five-year rest period before you come back again with bulbs. We did not want to get involved with horticultural crops as they would clash with the flower/bulbs needs so we opted for corn-growing as an alternative-break crop and the corn was used as feed rations for our poultry. In our last year of farming, we sold 763 tons of wheat to the new owner of our poultry unit from 200 acres. That was over the weighbridge, not over a pint of beer telling your neighbour what good crops you had. We adopted the one-pass method for cultivating, applying fertiliser and seed corn in one go very successfully. Our bigger tractors were well suited for this. Our air-assisted sprayer assured better coverage for bulb and corn crops at a much lower cost. We had our combine harvesters and grain-drier. Our business was thriving and running well.

For a long time, local gossip was that I was borrowing money from Germany at two and a half per cent. Although there was an enquiry at the time to prove this, wrong people want to believe it even today. I think it arose when a local farm came up for sale and I made arrangements with the bank manager to make a bid at the auction. The expected price was approximately £123,000. The day before auction the bank manager called at our farm and quietly informed me that my expected bid was too low. He also indicated he wanted me to have this farm as we had always kept our agreed terms. In this case, it was two per cent over base, repayable over three years. Eighteen per cent was a high interest rate, but the following year inflation reached twenty-six per cent for a while, so it was still a prudent investment. My assumption that the counter-bidder would bid £125,000 proved correct. My last bid of £125,500 secured the property.

The farm had good productive land, but untidy for our purpose. We did have a JCB and in our slack time converted the farm to the way we thought it should be. The farmhouse was no use to us, so we sold it for £47,000. Cropping for two years with daffodils made this investment self-financing with time to spare.

So on to the next project. Halgarrack Farm, with 120 acres and a nice farmhouse. Money was never my god. At best, it was only a yardstick to measure success, which I enjoy – and the challenge to succeed. Who doesn't play to win? Keeping in mind how difficult it was to accumulate my first £100.

The time has come to hand over to the next generation.

Andrew was twenty-five and our natural successor. Our eldest son, Stephen, was in the police force and never showed any real interest in farming. He seemed happy enough with his job. We were talking and living farming all and everyday so Andrew was a capable young farmer, running the business when we were on ever-increasing and longer holidays. While we were on a five-week tour of South America, arranged by SAGA the well-known tour operators, for the blue rinse and wrinklies, he realised he did not like living on his own. He even took his meals with our other son's family just across the road.

It still came as a surprise that he did not think himself capable and willing to take the responsibility of such a large business. Even my assurance that I was willing to make the transition gradually and willing to help in any way I could, or even reduce the size to any size he wanted, was not enough. His comment was that his intended would never make a farmer's wife – his words not mine. Disappointed – yes. But I must give Andrew full credit for his honesty.

Many farmers' sons would have taken over, unsure of their ability to succeed, and then make a mess of things. The next problem was: 'What next?' I would not consider taking on a manager. Still in charge and responsible was not my idea of retirement. So selling up was considered the best option. To appeal to any prospective purchaser with the necessary money it had to be as a going concern and we considered Savilles to be the best agents, as they had successfully sold a similar enterprise about four years earlier. Once it became known that our enterprise was coming up for sale, all the local papers became interested. The *Cornishman*, *West Briton*, *Western Morning News*, even the *Daily Telegraph* gave us a quarter-page on their front page. We gave them all our eight-page history of the family and the farm. All were free to print what they wanted. This was a great success. Even ITV and BBC came and filmed us for their local evening news at peak time. We were big news in the area.

Autobiography satisfies a certain curiosity. Through the book we enter the private world of somebody else, an unmentioned desire to be the fly on the wall.

The business was going well, but I was searching for more knowledge. As I had no formal horticultural education, I must agree with Bob Monkhouse when he said, 'Common sense without education is better than education without common sense.' Despite a limited education, I have always had an appetite for practical learning. All of which took me to Stoneleigh in the January of 1983 for a farm management course.

This farm management course was organised by the Agricultural Training Board for approved members of the agricultural community, a cross-section of the industry.

A manager of 10,000 acres from Lincolnshire, with a packing shed working twenty-four hours a day, and 200 employees; a partner of three pick-your-own farms; a turkey farmer with a large acreage, near Heathrow; the owner of a garden centre near London; a manager of a large estate belonging to a high-ranking military man – his duty to provide an income for the family and maintain the estate to a high standard; and a partner in two 250-cow dairy herds from Dorset; a land agent from Somerset; the manager of 500 breeding sows and offspring – a joint venture with a feed firm and Sainsbury's; the owner and managing director of 800 acres in general farming, plus 100 acres of daffodils; the manager of a large co-operative farm with retail dairy outlets and ambitions to add egg production; a large-scale soft fruit farm owner/manager from Worcester and Rudi Mock.

We were a mixed group. At the beginning, we were first introduced to the basic aims of management, its needs and its benefits.

It is necessary to stand back and see business as an integrated whole – rather than a collection of activities or enterprises. For this reason, the objectives of the business should be clarified. We must, therefore keep in mind the agreed objectives and interpret information when assessing what needs to be done.

This may be reading like a textbook but our tutors were instilling good business principles.

We moved on to business organisation. Here in Cornwall the overall authority was always mine. The buck stopped with me. I quite understand that in large enterprises, managers for this or that are necessary but I avoided this. Our business had never reached that size. The larger organisations suffer from overlapping, bypassing, frequently causing inefficiency and poor relationships.

Then came the business of staffing. We rely on people to get work done – to achieve results. They must be guided and given the opportunity to achieve their potential. This can be done by working with experienced staff, people passing on their skills. If this involves working in a gang, remember that the speed is very often set by the slowest. Every employee should be judged by his or her contribution, and rewarded accordingly.

Some tasks require a high degree of precision, tasks that are difficult to master – tasks that cannot easily be delegated. Poor selection will be detrimental to success, influencing flexibility and the deployment of staff.

There are two main approaches: one is watching for sore thumb indicators. Untidiness, tools not returned to the proper place – these are unacceptable.

The second approach is an examination of the technical, financial and human problems. All farm businesses are constantly employing new techniques, new machines, expanding production, raising output, streamlining their organisation and methods. The common aim is to increase labour efficiency. Ability levels and the range of skill required today demand a high level of technical knowledge and competence, and the right attitude. Tractor drivers for example are in charge of many thousands of pounds' worth of machinery today. The selection of the driver is vital.

This course provoked questions as well as providing answers. The effectiveness of staff in key skills, assessing new skills requirements. New machines. New techniques. Men tackling jobs for the first time. On our farm, the staff were extending areas of ability and knowledge. One of my best appointments was our number-one tractor driver. A smallholder himself, with agricultural training, he had served a mechanical apprenticeship with Massey Ferguson. He had the right attitude. He was the one we had been looking for.

In my business life, I have learned that learning can be costly – but by the application of job satisfaction, the process can be greatly improved. An effective business is dependent on competent people.

Much of life's learning can only take place on the job.

Now we came to the important subject of decision-making.

A large part of this course was spent working on members' own cases. We were invited to put forward three or four samples from our own business for discussion.

Would payment by result be better than a higher rate than average to discourage sloppy work? Piece-work for flower-picking was practised for many years and regarded as essential. Strict but fair supervision is necessary. Unsatisfactory bunches must be rejected. In the poultry unit, an above-average wage was adopted, as the welfare of the birds was of paramount importance.

What return per acre should be looked for to purchase land? Daffodils were our most important crop. Suitable land within reasonable distance from our base was essential. Daffodils are a high-cost, high-return crop; suitable land is of over-riding importance.

Is it cheaper to keep tractors and machinery until they are scrap? Or do you replace every two or three years? Our policy always was, if it is no more use to us, it would be of little use to anybody else either. We went for maximum discounts for payment on delivery. A small advertisement very often sold an article for more than it was worth. The discounts available can be quite considerable.

Would leasing over five to seven years be wiser than purchasing? I never liked the idea.

Marketing? With the progressive decline of commission agents and our increasing production, our marketing through Lingarden provided access to the markets world-wide. Economy of scale in production is necessary, and expertise in marketing world-wide is a specialist job.

So we came to financial objectives. I had to work for profits to service our existing commitments and ensure our expansion programme continued. I knew I had succeeded if the poultry unit maintained viability in the difficult climate. We needed the bulb returns to maintain their twenty per cent increase per year and the flower returns required an improvement of ten per cent.

Now we moved to production objectives: the crop reaching potential with growth not restricted through bad drainage, wheat infestation or disease.

Realistically we had to increase the output of eggs by three eggs per bird. Bulbs should be planted early and in good field conditions to obtain maximum lift. Elsewhere on the farm, we needed to obtain an average yield of no less than three tons of wheat per acre and all flowers were picked in the 'green' stage.

Finally, we came to personal objectives. I needed to delegate more responsibility, enabling me to enjoy life more by travelling around the world.

The goals were: to involve our son progressively in the running of the business and to take charge in my absence; eliminate all possible outside costs from the production of eggs; and purchase new exciting bulb varieties to maintain our position within the industry.

All that happened in 1983 and I look back with satisfaction that all aims were not only achieved, but surpassed in the following year, with enough money to spare, to fulfil my childhood dream of becoming the proud owner of a new Mercedes.

CHAPTER ELEVEN

A Daughter's Perspective

*H*ere is how our daughter Helene recalls growing up, and life on the farm – and her lifestyle today.

'Farming of any kind is never just a job but a whole way of life and most of my childhood memories focus on poultry and flowers.

'When I was born we were living in the cottage at Tredrea Farm, St Erth and although we left there when I was only three years old I have a very vivid image of life in that cottage. I was now aware of the hardships that were suffered by my parents, the fact that my mother had to carry all our water for cooking, etc. from the tap across the lane or that we had no electricity and had to go outside to the toilet. I do remember Father having his early morning wash with water from the rain-water tank outside the back door, even if he had to first break the ice on it in winter. To me this was normal.

'Because my father often worked a seven-day week, my mother picked the flowers we grew in the back garden and they bunched and packed them in the living room at night by gas light. The next day the farmer would take them to the station with his milk.

'I don't quite recall when the chickens arrived but there

was a wooden chicken house that I didn't like to go into because the hens pecked and flapped at me. In fact I have never liked chickens and cannot bear to pick them up, dead or alive. I didn't even like eating them as they always tasted tough and gamey and looked too much like dead birds to appeal to my appetite. The only part of the poultry business I liked was, in the beginning, when we had some day-old chicks and they were raised in brooders, under a lamp, with plenty of fresh wood-shavings. Even now, when I open a bag of fresh shavings to bed down the horses, the smell reminds me of the early days of chicken-rearing.

'I can look back on those early days and feel how cosy and self-contained they were. A bath in front of the fire, a cat that kept having kittens, jars full of flowers for market and a holly tree at Christmas because we couldn't afford anything else. Somehow, something of that was lost when we moved to Dixcarte.

'Dixcarte had been one of the three pubs in Crowan village in its mining heyday and the day we moved in it still had the benches in what had been the lounge, despite having closed its doors to customers some thirty years before. It was cold, draughty and spooky. Even to this day, I would not like to spend a night in there alone. The attic stairs were just outside my bedroom and many nights I lay in that room terrified to go to the bathroom because I had visions of ghostly figures lurking in the shadows.

'We still had the same jars of flowers waiting to be packed and the old wooden chicken house had moved with us but now things became frantic. There was so much to do and very little money for paid help, so both my parents worked long hours almost without rest, or so it seemed. By this time, my brother Stephen had been born and my grandmother was living with us. At least this meant that mother could work outside and have meals cooked and the children minded. My grandmother also used to help by washing and sorting eggs.

'As the business expanded we needed more help and so began a succession of lodgers who worked on the farm by day and had room and board as part of their wages. From the family point of view, this was not a very successful arrangement. Some were better than others but there were those who lodged in what should have been our dining room. (There were few arguments but at times my mother was pushed to the limit by their behaviour.) It was not an ideal solution, but a necessary inconvenience.

'Mostly we lived in the kitchen like most farmers, because it meant one could sit on the hard kitchen chairs in work-clothes and that was the room that had the television. In the evening, Father would do his paperwork at the kitchen table and on Fridays the workmen would come in at dinner-time for their wages. I have to say that most of the time I wished we could have lived in a normal house or on a proper farm with animals. I'm afraid I never really took to chickens or growing flowers. My mother always said that I was a Wednesday child: full of woe.

'As we grew older my brother and I started to do odd jobs on the farm to earn some money. When I was ten I desperately wanted riding lessons, so at weekends, in freezing cold weather, I picked violets – fifty tiny flowers to a bunch, thirty bunches to a box. It seemed to take forever. Father sent my box off to market and I received the money that it fetched. Sometimes it was only £1 per box but on a good day it would be thirty shillings, which seemed like a small fortune as riding lessons at that time were 7s 6d.

'Later, when we started farming the chickens in battery cages instead of using the deep litter method, I collected the eggs as well as making up the flower boxes. At various times in my life I returned home and there was always a job of some kind available. In the last years of the business, I did most of the book-keeping and secretarial work. It is quite a pity that these opportunities no longer exist for my children, who will now have to look outside the family to earn their pocket money.

'As the business grew and I got older and left home its significance in my life became less. Sometimes I feel a certain amount of regret that I never had the interest to continue with it myself but to succeed you have to be very single-minded and it was not something that I could get truly involved with.

'Growing up as a "foreigner" in Crowan in the 1950s was not easy. There were very few children to play with in the village at that time but somehow I used to amuse myself. Eleanor, who worked for my father used to let us watch children's programmes on her TV before we owned our own and Mrs Nicholls from the dairy let me talk to her while she sterilised the bottles. One of the best treats was when I was given a real pasty by one or other of the neighbours.

'Mother tried her best to cope with pasty-making but never quite got the hang of it. It was not until I went to school that I realised that I was different. Although I didn't know what a "Gerry" or a "Nazi" was, I understood that I was one. All of a sudden, life became more complicated. However, by the time I was about eleven most of the children got bored with name-calling and being half-German didn't seem to matter any more. I think Mother and Father found it hard to join in the social life of the local community as most of their friends were other Germans and their families, or ex-land army girls, none of whom we saw very often. Today there is certainly not a problem in being accepted locally, especially as there are so many newcomers to the village.

'Perhaps being seen as being different actually encouraged me to try to be different. I always had a taste for the exotic, which was fuelled by a calendar sent from one of the market wholesalers and featuring scenes from around the world. The year I was six the Taj Mahal was the view for October, my birthday month, and I began to inform everyone from my classmates to the school-dinner ladies that I was in fact born in India. This made a change for them from my tales of the lions and tigers we kept as pets at home and they duly acknowledged that this was indeed a point of great interest, and it influenced their attitude towards me. In fact in my early years, the most exotic my life got was the occasional trip to Germany to visit my father's family. This usually involved about two days cooped up in a car or van while we drove across Europe and resulted in me spending the first few days with my grandmother throwing up. Her remedy for this was camomile tea, the smell of which still makes me feel ill. Of course, our visits to Germany were not easy because of the language barrier. When I was about five years old father decided he was going to teach my mother and I to speak German. This was totally unsuccessful as my mother and I were not very good students. Therefore, communication with my relatives was extremely difficult.

'I did enjoy the early visits to Germany because my grandmother lived on what I thought of as a "proper" farm, with animals. The cows lived in stalls all the time but the largest of them was used to pull the cart out to the fields to collect hay. There was something magical about riding back to the house on top of a grass cart pulled by oxen and on later visits when a tractor had taken over that job I was terribly disappointed. Hay-making was also a painstaking job and one that I was not used to. The heat of a Bavarian summer is something I was not used to after the damp, temperate climate of Cornwall. Most of the time, whilst Father helped with turning the hay I was allowed to wander in the woods and collect wild strawberries and blueberries, or sit up on the high chairs used by the deer-hunters at the edge of the woods. I could climb up the ladder and get an excellent view over the local countryside. In the evenings, when it was cooler I helped my cousins stack the grass. It was back-breaking work and made me think perhaps it was better that we didn't have proper animals at home. The heat was so intense that we often had severe thunderstorms during the night, when my grandmother rounded us all up out of our beds in case the house caught fire. However, the bedding was certainly not designed for the hot summer nights – more the excessive cold of midwinter – as we were given goose-feather duvets at least a foot thick, which were unbearable and spent most of the night on the floor.

'I finally learned some German at school and even took a bilingual secretarial course but I am not a natural linguist and now would find it difficult to have any kind of conversation in that language. Consequently, I have not been to Germany for a visit since my grandmother died, over twenty years ago. I keep promising to take the children but have never made it yet.

'At twenty-three I finally made it to university – The School of Oriental and African Studies in London. Here my horizons were considerably broadened and my travel plans finally lived up to my dreams. I had never made a good secretary but these skills were invaluable to me during the long hot vacations as I could earn very good money temping. By working for several weeks, I could save enough to travel beyond the bounds of Europe. At the end of my first year, in 1977, I joined a group working on an Israeli Kibbutz where we had to pick apples and work in the kitchens. This was certainly a different kind of experience. Situated on the border with Lebanon, the night was punctuated by loud bursts of gunfire as the Israeli soldiers billeted on the kibbutz took pot shots at the Lebanese and vice versa. I suppose it was quite dangerous, especially as a few years later we learned that the kibbutz had been raided and one member killed. At the time though it had seemed like a normal way to live. The friends I made on that trip have stayed friends ever since and indeed, that was where I first met my husband, David.

'The following summer I saved to join a tour of East and Central Africa and, lastly, following my graduation in 1979, David and I took off for a year in the USA. We had £1,000 each and a one-way ticket to San Francisco but somehow managed to find jobs in various states and travel the length and breadth of the country, including a month in Mexico. We travelled until we were literally down to our last pennies and arrived back in England with £6 between us, from where we had to begin re-building our lives back here.

'My working life has always been rather without structure or form. For girls in Cornish schools in the 1960s choices were very restricted – mostly due to the teachers' lack of imagination and the premise that we would all just get married and raise families. Having tried secretarial work and hated it, I thought teaching might be the answer. An attempt at the PGCE in Exeter proved that this was not going to be so. Marriage and a return to Cornwall were not a wise career move either and eventually I was working back at the farm, which also fitted in with being a mother. Crèche facilities were provided on site and I could work in the office while my mother minded the children, which was an ideal arrangement.

'My career took an unexpected turn when my youngest brother decided not to take on the family business and father decided to retire. The result of this was that I had a gift from my parents that was given to me to invest and I did this by buying several properties that I let as bedsits. Life as a landlady could probably fill a book by itself and is certainly not without its trials. What it has succeeded in doing though is providing me with a flexible job that can be fitted in around the family, providing us with a good living. Perhaps I should have taken a degree in psychology instead of geography although I don't think anything can prepare you for the shock of dealing with the problems of letting rooms. Naïve I certainly was but after ten years I have learned to take the bad with the good and know that however awkward a tenant may be, in time they move on – possibly with all your furniture – but at least out of your hair. I have managed to acquire a good batch of tenants over the years but I am always aware that a bad one is lurking just around the corner and will catch me out if I become too complacent. It's a bit like living next to a dormant volcano. You never know when it will erupt!

'For years while the family was young, travel was again restricted to Europe, mostly somewhere warm, with a beach. Now they are growing up I have managed to venture further afield and have branched out into Asia. In 1997, I had a taste of Vietnam when I joined a group travelling from Hanoi to Ho Chi Minh City (Saigon) by train. Last year some friends and I organised a visit to Burma and now we have started up an enterprise importing textiles and lacquerware, which will, of course mean we have to travel regularly to negotiate with our suppliers. This is my idea of heaven.

'Horses have been my other passion – one shared by my mother and daughter but not my father. Father has a typical farmer's view of horses, that they are not useful and cost a lot of money; anybody who is involved with horses usually neglects their other business because the horses take priority. I cannot argue against this but what's life for if you can't do the things you enjoy? Somehow I have managed to accumulate four horses, which is probably two too many but they are easier to acquire than get rid of. Now most of my weekends are spent at horse shows with my daughter and her horse Orbit Jack – Oojie to her. I am a little envious as we go off with the trailer to pony club rallies and suchlike and watch her fly over jumps that I now feel too vulnerable to tackle. I was fifteen by the time I had my first horse and as neither Mother nor Father knew anything about them it was not a successful experience because we ended up with something entirely unsuitable. Nevertheless, I do enjoy being part of the horse scene at the moment and it will probably come to an end when Charlotte goes off to university in a few years. My son Alex is unfortunately not so keen on our equestrian activities and wants to spend his time surfing – an activity I do not enjoy in the least.

'My life is rooted in Cornwall but rather than wanting to become Cornish I would prefer to think of myself as a "global" person, not necessarily restricting myself to any particular nationality. Home is where family and friends are and for me that could be anywhere. The main advantage of staying in one place for any length of time is that you build up a network of contacts – useful when looking for a reliable plumber or electrician. I now look forward to a time when I will be free to travel the world, hopefully while I am still young enough to have a sense of adventure.'

1 *Rudi's birthplace in Germany.*

2 *Rudi on the right with his mother and family. The small boy is an evacuee from the Ruhr. 1941*

3 Rudi in working service in the South of France – aged seventeen.

4 Rudi and colleagues swearing in for working service.

5 Rudi with members of the Lelant Chess Club.

6 Rudi in deep concentration at the chess board.

7 *Tredrea Cottage 1951–57.*

8 *Workers on Rudi's flower farm*

9 *The working face of Rudi's flower farm –*
picking Golden Ducat.

10 *Flower-pickers at work.*

11 *Inside the poultry house.*

12 *The deep litter house.*

13 Opposite, top, Connie in Land Army uniform.

14 Opposite bottom left, Rudi standing outside Tredrea Cottage: 'our first home'.

15 Opposite bottom right, An earlier photograph: Connie and Rudi on their wedding day in London.

16 Above, Another earlier photograph: broccoli planting at Tredrea with Wilfred Harry at the wheel.

17 Below: The wedding group.

18   Rudi in Cornwall in 1949 – ambitions growing.

19   Rudi and Connie's three children and the much loved dog.

Chapter Twelve

Shirley Looks Back on Forty Years

It is sometimes said business and friendship do not mix. Shirley Glasson who worked for me demolishes that theory. Here is how Shirley, a Cornish girl, remembers our relationship – and work on the farm.

'It was 1957 when we first met Rudi. I was born in Crowan and at that time the village was one large family. Everyone knew each other – not only as neighbours, but as friends. Now Crowan was taken by surprise, an empty house had new occupants arriving: a German gentleman with his London-born wife and family. Now to us "country bumpkins" London was the other end of the world, and as for Germany that was something totally different.

'I don't expect at that time anyone living in Crowan had been further afield than Plymouth. At first people didn't understand Rudi's accent but I must say personally I always understood what he said, and as time went by and I worked for him I understood better. I always remember Rudi worked very hard in the field, with a trilby hat on his head and when he came in for meals he would bang the hat against the gatepost to get rid of the dust. That hat took some punishment.

'We lived at the other end of the village and about twelve o'clock we would hear Connie calling Rudi to come in for his dinner as their field was at the bottom of our back garden. As time went on the calls got less and I understand the dinners were on the table for whatever time he arrived.

'When Rudi and Connie came to Crowan there was only one chicken house, and more followed later. I started working at Dixcarte two afternoons a week. The chickens were in deep litter, someone used to pick up the eggs and they were brought up to a small packing shed to be cleaned and packed in boxes of thirty dozen.

'Then came a Hatch House – a house full of hens in cages, something we had never seen before. They really did look happy and contented. Gradually came more poultry houses and several ladies and myself picked up the eggs every day and teenagers used to work at weekends for pocket money. They were paid one penny for a tray of thirty eggs. That was the old penny when there were 240 in a pound, not decimal money. At that time, this was considered very good pay.

'One day Andrew missed the school bus so he thought he would come home and pick up the eggs. He worked out how much money he had earned. It was quite a shock for him when Rudi didn't pay up. 'You were supposed to be at school today.'

At the time I don't think Andrew really liked school, but he never missed that school bus again – it was a lesson he didn't forget.

'Then progress crept in – so we thought. Two poultry houses were converted with trays at the end of the rows and belts installed to bring the eggs up through the house on to the trays. We thought it wonderful at first. We didn't foresee the problems which followed when one egg would break or a soft-shell egg would run down the tray making one big mess – but that is progress.

'We had our good times and bad. There was a fire in one of

122

the two poultry houses at the bottom of the field – a very sad day indeed. One occasion like that is enough for a lifetime.

'Farmers in the neighbourhood would come with dung-spreaders and slurry tankers to take away the poultry manure to spread on their land. Sometimes if the spreader was too full or the manure a little on the wet side it would spill on to the road especially if the tractors were going downhill, and quicker than a blink of the eye it would be reported and someone would have to brush up the road.

'Rudi then phased out the poultry units at Crowan and moved to Tremayne. When flower-time came I used to help in the packing shed. Four to six women would come to help when required to bunch. When picked they had to be bent over like a goose's neck, not tight as they are picked today.

'At the time Rudi packed all the flowers, we were only allowed to bunch.

'There were three tables in the shed – one for packing and the other two for bunching and making the flower boxes. At weekends Helene, Stephen and Andrew would make the boxes ready for the packing. They would rush out in the morning to see who could get the best stapler – one was always better than the other two – and sometimes there were tears.

'When packing flowers Connie would go indoors to turn her Sunday joint, and when she came back she brought with her the smell of her roast dinner.

'All that was left for us was wondering how our dinner was getting on – we left our husbands with instructions and times – they did a very good job watching the clock: time to put potatoes in the oven – time to put carrots on.

'Sometimes if the flowers weren't looking as good as they should the bunch would come flying across the shed. After a while we learned to "duck" quite quickly. We wondered how Rudi knew who had bunched them. It wasn't until we were promoted to packing ourselves did we understand.

'Once the flowers were packed, came the loading of the van, which sometimes was a nightmare. Rudi had a Morris 1000 van. Loading the van was like putting a quart of milk in a pint jug. He used to fill the van, have wood extensions hanging out of the back door, on the roof – everywhere possible. Rudi bought a small field from a Mr Hubbard that was very damp and grew lovely Arum lilies. They used to be cut, cleaned inside of the flower with a toothbrush and packed singly.

'We used to cut pittisporum and wrap it in hessian bags to send away. We bunched kaffir lilies – which we called pepper lilies because they used to make us sneeze. We also bunched chincherinchees that lasted for several weeks. I had a cousin home from South Africa one year and he said they grew wild where he lived. We did an experiment in colouring them. We stood them in coloured water and the flowers changed colour, but it wasn't a success. We bunched alstromeria too, which was a very pretty flower – red, orange and yellow, but it brought everyone who touched it out in a very itchy rash.

'Then Rudi bought more land which meant more flowers and more staff and, of course, the little packing shed wasn't big enough. So there was a new one built with tanks to sterilise the bulbs, big store rooms, cool for the flowers, or warm for the bulbs.

'At one stage, there were about 100 women bunching flowers. It was then that about six of us were promoted to packing. What a great honour we thought at the time that Rudi would trust us to pack his precious flowers.

'Bunches came in all shapes – mostly ten in a bunch if we were lucky. Some never got to bunch as we would like. I think they just came out for a day off housework, husbands and children. We watched these ladies come in the packing shed to see Rudi for a job. Some wanted picking – some bunching. Some came dressed in their Sunday best. We could tell when they came in the door, the women dressed in old anoraks and wellington boots were the ones who got a job, not dressed as one lady was – a fur coat and high-heeled shoes. She didn't think daffodils grew in fields, she thought they grew in greenhouses with cement paths all around. Needless to say, she didn't stay long.

'Rudi used to keep a book with names of people who worked there. We always wondered why some names had letters after their names, such as NBG which was 'No bloody good!' I never did get to know what letters he put after my name. I think Rudi thought I talked too much. Perhaps I did talk too much, but there was one day when he shut me up.

'The television cameras arrived, and we didn't know they were coming. I think if we knew no one would have turned up for work that day. I wished that the floor would open up, but we got through the morning. When it was shown on TV my granddaughter asked me why I didn't wave to her. That was the last thing on my mind that day!

'Some days while bunching flowers during the winter, and it was very cold, some women would faint – they soon came round after a cup of tea.

'When we moved to the big packing shed the hand staplers were replaced with electric ones, and boys would come up from the village of Praze to make boxes for the next day. The boxes would be lined with blue paper and white paper for the blue iris.

'We used to cover little wood "sticks" with spikes each end with paper which were used as "spreaders" to stop the flowers moving in transit. These were replaced with metal ones. One Whitsun, Rudi and I worked all day bunching iris, and as fast as we bunched the gypsies who used to come and buy flowers to sell on their "pitches" at the corner of the streets in near by towns, bought them all.

'As time went on the flowers were picked and bunched in the fields, and the pickers were paid by the bunch instead of by the hour. Children who worked in the fields were paid by their age and sometimes there would be some dispute over their real age. One boy even brought his birth certificate with him when Rudi thought he wasn't as old as he said he was.

'When picking up bulbs during the summer holidays children used to come to work and every day women who worked at Dixcarte used to take a turn – one day a week to supervise the children – not a pleasant task at times. After the bulbs were harvested, four of the women staff went on the grader. We used to go home very dusty and dirty, but came back again next day and every day until they were finished.

'When the large lorries from Rowe and Co came to collect the bulbs that were sold, they had a fruit and vegetable business as well: we would order nectarines and the lorry driver would bring them. Working in the dust all day, they really went down a treat.

'When I started work for Rudi I used to milk our cows before I went to Dixcarte. We would be up at five-thirty a.m. every day, would start work at eight a.m., leave at four-thirty p.m. which was milking time again, and if Rudi was very busy we would carry on again in the evening. We were six regular packers, plus Rudi and Connie. Yes, we were working most of all for the money which gave us the "extras". I always said that our cows provided the bread and butter and working for Rudi provided the jam.

'Connie used to go to the bank every Friday to get money for the wages. The money used to be spread out on the kitchen table. The security was second to zero. Later the staff were paid out in the fields every day. When selling eggs to customers, if I needed change, I would go indoor to "help myself" from the money tin.

'I can truthfully say we were as one happy family and we are still good friends.

'Of course, when packing the flowers in tight bud there were times when a difference of opinion would arise as to what variety of daffodils we were packing.

'When Rudi retired, we retired as well, but Rudi and Connie

now living at Praze brought back many memories for me. Where he built his new home was once Praze Railway Station, and I used to go to school at Helston on the train that went from Gwinear Road to Helston.

'It is like our school song, "Forty Years On", but Rudi and Connie, I can truly say, are still good friends to us.'

CHAPTER THIRTEEN

Daffodils

*D*affodils are among the best-loved flowers. They bring lovely splashes of colour into our homes and gardens. Their delightful golden tones can brighten the greyest, the dullest of days.

Daffodils too are among the most versatile of flowers and, along with roses, they must be the most photographed and painted flowers in all horticulture. The traditional wide mouth trumpet of the daffodil is still hugely popular – though, over the years, numerous different shapes have been developed and grown. They have a stunning colour range from reds and pinks to the pure white narcissus. Daffodils, in their magical way, symbolise spring and all its glory and promise – though, of course, here in Cornwall, I soon discovered, you can get daffodils very early in the year.

As long ago as 1807 daffodils inspired the poet William Wordsworth to write:

> I wandered lonely as a cloud
> That floats on high o'er vales and hills,
> When all at once I saw a cloud,
> A host, of golden daffodils:

Beside the lake, beneath the trees,
Fluttering and dancing in the breeze.

Another fine poet, John Masefield, wove the flower into one of his poems entitled 'The West Wind':

It's a warm wind, the west wind, full of birds' cries;
I never hear the west wind but tears are in my eyes.
For it come from the west lands, the old brown hills,
And April's in the west wind, and daffodils.

In Cornwall, daffodils invariably feature strongly in our flower shows. One of the best known is held at St John's Hall, Penzance. Growers and exhibitors, of course, have different views and different theories about the cultivation of flowers – listening to them can be an interesting and sometimes a confusing experience. This is not altogether surprising because a good bloom is not easily classified. What may be considered an ideal bloom for floral art or in a garden may not equal the requirements of showing purposes. There is no doubt flowers and daffodils in particular are very much part of the Cornish scene.

A bulb gives the impression of being dormant from summer through to the days of autumn but that is only a superficial impression. In reality, important changes are taking place inside the bulb and the care given to the bulbs during the time it is out of the ground is important – that care and attention will be rewarded in the long-term by the flower production.

Interpreters of dreams say that if we dream of daffodils then we can forget any worries and if, in our dream, we see daffodils growing in a field or a garden we are destined for a happy successful future.

This is not altogether wishful thinking either because for centuries dreams have been regarded as more than pure superstition. Learned men and women have studied and investigated dreams and there have been many instances of dreaming turning out to be 'events casting their shadows before them'.

Daffodils are beautiful flowers and nowhere else in the world will you see so many as here in West Cornwall. The period February, March, April, the whole area looks as if it is suffering from yellow fever. You admire the beautiful scenery but there is another side to this pretty picture.

It means that the grower has failed to benefit from their commercial value as cut flowers. Once the flower has started to open that opportunity has gone.

There are various reasons why this happens. A major hurdle is finding suitable pickers for such short seasonal work. While a long cool period in January/March would be ideal to regulate supply and demand, a day or two of misty, drizzly rain coming from the south-west will upset the best plans. In January and February, there is a good demand in America and the Continent apart from British requirements.

Supply and demand retains the balance at good prices. A sudden mild spell will upset the picture and lack of suitable pickers is usually the biggest problem. Twelve years ago, many housewives were looking for seasonal employment to earn a little extra. Schoolchildren from fourteen years upwards were regulars for Saturdays and Sundays, earning some money for the first time in their lives. I still recall many of their smiling faces when they received their pay in the evenings. Today many of the pickers come from Eastern Europe, organised and employed by gang masters. Good money can be earned by those willing to put up with the weather.

For me, working with daffodils has been the most satisfying and most rewarding part of my life. When it became clear our youngest son did not wish to take over the business and all the responsibility, it was a bitter disappointment and the sale of part of our business inevitable. I could not bear to part with all my daffodils and keeping the most promising to multiply for another five years as a hobby proved highly profitable. Selling them was my retirement number two. It became a habit with me. To stop all this nonsense I gifted the remainder of my hobby collection to our grandchildren: some three hundred varieties in total, some only a dozen, others half a hundredweight. Two hundred and sixty-four are first seeding crosses and so far completely unselected.

There is a one-fifth share in CABGA (Cornish Area Bulb Growers Association) 2000 in crosses selected from the best earlier crosses at Rosewarne, flowering from October onwards. I don't think I shall live long enough to see them in commercial production. If our grandchildren are interested in daffodil growing, they will be a start with the most up-to-date varieties. In the meantime, I have their permission to rogue out any which I think not good enough – and destroy them. An enquiry from an American growers' representative from Washington and Oregon, the only two states suitable for daffodil-growing in America, regarding availability of foundation breeding stock, gives a pleasant feeling that we have something others would like to have.

While there may still be room for expansion for the early varieties coming on the market in January and February, this demand has been met by the greenhouse growers in the past. I recall a phone call at five o'clock in the morning by the leading Covent Garden wholesaler saying, 'Rudi, what have you sent us today?' I knew he was referring to the six boxes of 'Barrenwyn'. He was so excited about these – a new variety we had purchased from the Rosewarne Experimental Station and held the total stock. It features very much now in the exports to the USA and is a serious competitor to the forced greenhouse production. It is a quality flower with strong resistance to bulb diseases.

The international daffodil checklist had 23,000 listed named varieties in 1991, divided into ten divisions:

1	Trumpet
2	Large cupped
3	Small cupped
4	Double
5	Triandros
6	Cyclomineus
7	Jonquilla – scented
8	Tazetta – scented
9	Poeticus
10	Wild species

This does not include the 150 tested varieties I have passed on to our grandchildren and the others untested. With the housewife showing an increasing interest in fragrant flowers, the Jonquilla type has taken my fancy.

Daffodils were not only a very profitable enterprise, I did really enjoy working with them. This also applies to Mr Paul Clark, the gentleman who bought our business when I retired in 1990. I became aware of this when Paul and his wife inspected my seedlings after the Experimental Breeding Station at Rosewarne closed down. He must have found the exceptionally high prices he obtained selling his Winchester Bulb Company down here irresistible and, as a result, purchased 7,500 acres of prime land in Lincolnshire and entered large-scale farming and created a new bulb enterprise at Nocton, Lincolnshire. I always thought he would be back growing daffodils again in Cornwall and now he has done just that.

An article in the *Farmers Weekly* in February 2000 is further proof that Paul Clark has made his mark. When the writer visited and monitored the fortunes of his host farm of 'Cereals 2000' he found flower production in Cornwall provided more satisfaction than large-scale arable farming in Lincolnshire. The writer stated it is quite something when cut flowers from two hundred acres in Cornwall make more in a month than 7,500 acres of arable cropping made last year, especially when the cut flowers are only a bi-product of the bulb-growing operation. The key to his year's success was his £1.25 million investment in new earlier flowering varieties, flowering up to five weeks earlier than the industry's standard 'Golden Harvest'.

At Spalding Flower Show there was talk about the 'new boy'. Paul is not a new boy to daffodils. The arable part of his enterprise is new to him. In future, he will produce daffodils from December onwards in his new automated and temperature-controlled greenhouses in Lincolnshire, and, of course, early daffodils in West Cornwall.

For many farmers, diversification is simply unrealistic. They not only do not have enough money but they do not want to take the radical step of getting out now. Historically, land prices follow the industry four or five years later. So the farmhouse could well be worth more than the rest of the farm. With the difficulties the farming industry is experiencing, banks and landlords are adopting a more realistic attitude, allowing farmers to part with possession of the land on short-term leases, whereby up to ten per cent of the land value is obtainable for a yearly rent and, in many cases, payment is in advance. I have had the privilege of Paul showing me his growing stock down here and I must say they look very good. We both share the view that there is a good future for the multiplication of the virus-free seedlings and disease-resistant new stocks.

CHAPTER FOURTEEN

Jennifer's Story – Another Worker Recalls the Problems and the Pleasures of Life with Daffodils

I have been working for Rudi for twenty-one years as an irregular or part-time worker. There have been many changes in that time. I started out bunching daffodils in a huge shed, tables squeezed into every corner; at least eight people at each table, and if really busy, more pushed in. The bunches had to be just so, all stems had to be level, heads pretty much the same. If there were untidy bunches, Rudi or the other packers seemed to know from which table the bunches came. The offending table or single person concerned, would be again shown how the bunches should be made up.

'If this persisted, there would be a shouted remark, followed by the offending bunch sailing through the air: a clear warning that sloppiness would not be tolerated. Some workers said that Rudi had eyes in the back of his head, or another part of his anatomy. He knew who came in late or left early, who was always going to the toilet to have a smoke – just to waste time. He knew what was going on. At busy times like Mothering

Sunday or Easter, some of the pickers from the field would come in to help bunch. On the last sending day, Rudi wanted the cold stores empty to cash in on the higher prices for these special days.

'It may seem strange that pickers did not like coming indoors to do bunching. They would rather be outside in all weathers than standing still on the concrete floor. We guarded our jobs jealously, and were glad to see the back of them. We thought they must be nuts, outside it was far colder, apart from the wind and rain. Mostly, the ladies outside came with plenty of warm clothing and wellies on. If a new face came through the door, everyone had a quick look to see what they were wearing. We have seen all sorts – short skirts and stockings, high-heeled shoes, white fur fabric coats. Rubber gloves were a must. They helped to keep the hands dry and warm, but mainly the daffodil sap can bring you out in an awful rash – not only on the hands and face but also on parts that don't see the light of day.

'When you were chosen to bunch some of Rudi's 'specials', such as 'Planet' or a few others, that was promotion. When you were asked to help with the packing, you had reached the top. Rudi was really fussy about presentation. He said if a prospective buyer sees an untidy pack he had every right to expect that quality of the contents is no better and would be foolish to pay more than the lower end of the market price for the day.

'All this bunching in the shed soon came to an end as Rudi changed, in common with other growers, to pick and bunch in the field. Rudi's pay was usually half a pence better than most, but this had to be earned. He always demanded a better quality of work than most. Actually there was good money to be made with practice. A good picker could pick upwards of 1,600 bunches in an eight-and-a-half-hour day: ten flowers per bunch, stems level at the bottom, with a rubber ring doubled up to hold the bunch secure. Many had reached their day's wages – hourly rate – by lunch time. They would never do the same in the afternoon. One always slowed down after lunch.

'I supervised outside. My job was to see that everybody was doing their job right, checking their count and recording everybody's numbers. Any newcomers had to be shown how. For the 'home market' a little colour was permitted, but not too much. For 'export' all had to be absolutely green and the bud straight up – pencil straight is the trade description. Golden Ducat and Planet were different. They had to be picked up in what we call showing between five and ten past on the clock. When the sheath had split sufficiently to see a little colour and ten past the hour before the head had turned at the right angle. If you were to pick these two varieties earlier, they would never open in a vase.

'Very often I heard somebody shouting across the field, "Jen, can you come and measure my flowers?" I always had a 14" stick marked off at 12" so I could keep an eagle eye on the lengths. Anything shorter were thrown out and not paid for – a real waste of time and flowers. The daffodil season started for a few of us before Christmas: at first, not every day, but soon seven days a week and in ever increasing numbers, until April and a few again in May. Daffodils don't seem to know the days of the week, so the longest I worked without a break was eight weeks. In the early days, we took on youngsters from fourteen upwards at weekends. Some were very willing to learn and were good. Others just thought that the hours only brought dollars. Rudi always said, "Encourage the good ones. They will be our future pickers." Like the rest, every bad bunch was not paid for. The daffodil-pickers were a hardy breed. The waterproofs kept them reasonably dry and helped to keep the wind out. The mud was sometimes deep enough to suck your boots off. Pouring rain, no shelter, coffee made cold and weak with the rain. When you started moving about, you soon felt warmer again. At peak times, Rudi had other supervisors working in other fields as well, probably picking other varieties. When workers came in the morning, everyone was given a card that had to be filled in with name and address, and I had to enter the numbers picked and sign the cards. Everyone was paid in cash, whenever that person chose to leave. No signature, no money. I also had to keep track so people would give their correct name and address for DHSS purposes. Any stranger coming into the field was always thought to be someone from the DHSS and those who were still collecting their dole were bending their backs lower and hiding their faces deep under their oiled hood – until he had gone again.

'Bulbs are also part of the daffodil cycle in June and July. Certainly more back-breaking than daffodil-picking. I personally have had no problem with either. Everyone hoped for decent weather. Those who can take the sun were out in shorts and sun-tops. Oh, what a lovely tan! Rudi said he paid us to pick up the bulbs and getting brown was a bonus. When it was really wet we had to wait for a day for the bulbs to dry off. All bulbs were put straight in half-ton boxes, which was better than having to heave about heavy nets, quicker too.

'All the years I have been working for Rudi I have found him a fair, considerate employer, and I think most of us felt part of team where good work was appreciated and fairly rewarded. I think I am also speaking for many others I meet occasionally in town, when I say that Rudi was the best employer I have ever worked for.'

CHAPTER FIFTEEN

Praze Station & Poultry

We used Praze Station in our early days when we had only small quantities of flowers, and Frank James, the man in charge, could take them indoors when it was raining or cover them with a plastic sheet. As our quantities increased this would have been impractical, so Dr Beeching's closure of the line did not create any difficulty for us as a business. In fact, the eventual sale turned out to our advantage. The Railway Board in Bristol examined several possible alternative uses, such as industrial development – but without success.

Villages are often hives of gossip and our village of Praze is no exception. Such gossip is sometimes used for a purpose and this was the case with Praze Station.

A small local developer, keen on acquiring the station, went around saying, 'Have you heard the council has bought the old station?'

I was suspicious; so much so I telephoned Bristol.

'Has Praze Station been sold?' I enquired.

'Praze Station has not been sold,' came the crystal-clear reply.

This local man had been deliberately spreading rumours in the hope of killing off any other bids for the old station.

With our intention to relocate our poultry units, the railway line would provide the best possible access road to it. A complaint to British Rail that the fences were no longer stock-proof where the line went through our land, and pointing out that we would hold them responsible for any claim arising from that neglect, brought the desired response. They made us an offer to sell them the four and a half acres for £450. An offer for nine-tenths of a mile of ready-made road to connect the Crowan Road just south side of Praze with the B3303 Camborne-Helston Road was too good to refuse. It still left us approximately 100 feet short from the end of the line to the main road, which was part of the station. The sale of this area had been in the air for the previous two years. To encourage them finally to reach a decision, I made the purchase of the line conditional that the sale of the station would materialise soon, and at best offer received. It was a calculated risk. The line would be of no use to anybody else, and to maintain the fences would be expensive. I had an idea that the offer by another interested party had come up to £4,000, which was not accepted, and the invitation to a final offer would most likely be a nice and round £5,000, which I later found out was spot on. So, a little above this sum secured it: an excellent deal for us, especially as our planning application for our new poultry unit at Tremayne was already in progress. We knew there would be opposition, as a neighbouring poultry farmer had used a manure dryer for the manure, which made life for those people close by very unpleasant.

Our planned unit completely eliminated the smell and had worked very successfully in the Liskeard area. I invited councillors to come with me and see for themselves. I requested permission to explain to the parish council our intention but the request was refused whereas the local doctor's wife was allowed to give her reasons why it should be refused. The lady collected 120 signatures against our proposal and the opposition was formidable. I needed all the help I could get so I employed a planning specialist with experience of how planning committees work. The development proposed was close to the hamlet of Tremayne, which provided the strongest objection. My suggestion to the specialist to move the unit a little further away to another field was rejected by him with the remark, 'Not yet.' His opinion was that if we proposed to move it two miles from there we would still get objections. But the people from the hamlet would later be grateful for every 100 yards. We moved away from them because agricultural buildings proved very difficult to be refused at the time. A meeting with all the objectors, the council and ourselves under the Chairmanship of Councillor Moyle was held at Praze Institute. Some very wide assumptions were made, amongst others that forty-foot lorries would call every day with day-old chicks, while our proposal would only require a Ford transit van, three times a year for that purpose. They obviously did not realise that the chairman was a highly respected intelligent farmer. The debate went on for some time but the strongest objection made by most people was that a large, exaggerated number of lorries would continuously pass Praze School and it would be inevitable that a number of children would be killed. After a thorough debate, the chairman invited me to give my opinion. Having listened to the objections, many of which were unjustified, or exaggerated, I felt that had the parish council granted me the courtesy of explaining my side of the application, most of the arguments and objections would not have arisen.

The most important issue concerned the safety of the children – and the route.

The obvious question came: 'Which way do you intend to get there?'

'Along the railway line.'

'Have you got permission?'

'No, I don't need it.'

'Have you an arrangement with them?'

'I've bought the railway line.'

There was a long silence.

The chairman, closing the meeting, said, 'A decision will be made after our January meeting.'

We responded by saying, 'If the closeness of the unit to Tremayne is a major concern, we are willing to put it in a neighbouring field, a little further away.'

This was agreed, with a planning sub-committee and the application altered accordingly. The January planning meeting was intended to approve this amended application. As it is customary that Councillor for the Area's opinion will be taken into account, it does appear that after all the promises made he did not want to be part of the decision to grant approval, so he did not turn up. The decision was postponed until the February meeting. The approval was granted in February, but surprise, surprise, it was for the field originally objected to and not the site agreed with the sub-committee as the better alternative.

The chairman of the planning committee couldn't believe what he had just signed. A request to return the signed approval was agreed in return for a signed statement that the new application would be granted. As it was not forthcoming, I gave the council notice that if it was not received by a stated date we would start building as if approval was granted. I cannot recall the details now twenty-five years later, but the Chief Planning Officer at the time, Mr Nicholls, called and the final siting was agreed and the position regarding the people living in Tremayne was the major consideration.

Outline planning permission was granted in field no 1347 for a domestic bungalow. The previous owner had promised a wedding gift to his neighbour, four years after he had sold the farm to us. I was not pleased that he acted without consulting me first. There was also no access to the site. The only access at the time would have been through the farmyard, which was totally unacceptable.

When we later applied for detailed approval, we were informed that the original outline approval was not valid. Our solicitor confirmed that it was. The planning authorities stated that the detailed application was out of date, when this was clearly not the case. A further attempt was that we had no access. We clearly had, but the applicant had not. When I finally wrote to Kerrier, this was now a matter of principle and not favours for some. Permission was granted without any conditions attached.

Planning applications frequently generate a lot of hot air. Michael Heseltine MP said, 'A planning application should be decided "on its merits".'

But, too often, local politics come into such matters.

'He's a local boy who deserves something...'

'He's a good boy...'

And the other side of this coin is when a parish councillor asks, 'Hasn't he got enough yet?'

So I refused to sell him the plot and offered him a third-of-an-acre plot with access to the Praze–Blackrock road as an alternative. It was an isolated site in open country, with panoramic views from Porthleven to St Michael's Mount, Penzance to St Ives. He raised some doubt whether he would get planning permission there. I told him that with the friends he had, he should get it – without problems. And he did precisely that. So, I sold him the plot for £60. It must be the cheapest building plot ever sold in the West Country.

With the sale of the poultry units, the ex-railway line became a necessity for the new owners of the poultry farm at Tremayne. Had I just granted access rights, the upkeep responsibility would still rest with me and collecting for the maintenance would be a consistent worry. So I gifted it to the new owners and retained unrestricted access over it. After all, it is in daily use by twenty-five-ton lorries and only in 1999 was major repair work needed.

CHAPTER SIXTEEN

🌱

Grandfather Talks to Grandson

It was a beautiful day with just a gentle breeze blowing from the west – our prevailing wind direction. It comes straight off the Atlantic, only about six or seven miles from St Ives and Hayle.

This was a day too good to spoil by doing work. After all what is a nice garden really for? It's there to be enjoyed. I have done very little gardening in this the last year of the twentieth century. Three weeks before Easter 1998 I had a slight stroke. Luckily for me the ambulance men made a quick correct decision taking me to Penzance where they knew I should receive immediate attention. Had I been taken to Truro there might have been some delay and I might not now be writing these words. Yes, the hospital at Penzance looked after me very well and I have made a complete recovery. Complete? Well, almost!

So as the first millennium drew to its close, I have resisted the temptation of using spade and hoe in the argument with the weeds. Instead, I have done my arguing with carefully applied weedkiller. Our garden has sufficiently matured to be ready for this more leisurely weed control. As the weeds have not been allowed to grow, the shrubs have spread in ever-increasing circles preventing the weeds from living under them. It has done an almost perfect job.

A garden is often a good place in which to think and talk. James Turner, that very good writer who lived his last years in North Cornwall, once said, 'The record of a man's gardening is the autobiography if not of his soul, certainly of his body.' As a young man, James Turner fell out with his mother's gardener and learnt an early important lesson: '…what a man plants is his own, even if his weeds can be claimed by another.'

Admittedly today the lawn could do with a haircut but I was not in the mood. The fluffy clouds moved in an easterly direction and in some curious way my thoughts drifted with them – almost as if they are carrying greetings from me to the country where I was born. Suddenly, though, my thoughts were shattered by the crunching noise of our daughter coming along the gravel drive in her four-wheel drive. It is always good to see our children and grandchildren. Helene and Charlotte disappeared into the house searching for their grandma. Alex, our eldest grandson, came in my direction. Heidi, our faithful canine companion, lying beside my feet stirred and went to meet him.

'Hallo, Granddad, having a nice rest?'

'No Alex, I am just sitting and thinking and watching the clouds drifting across the sky. Later on today these same clouds will be over the country where I was born.'

Alex looked thoughtful: 'I wonder if Uncle Albert will see them…'

That was an interesting thought.

Heidi was now back in her normal place slightly in front of me, her big brown eyes on me.

Turning to Alex again I said, 'Your mother always says she will take you there to meet your cousins. I am sure she will do that one day. As your sister Charlotte is learning German at school she can do all the talking and translating. Your mother seems to have forgotten what German she learned years ago.

'You have seen photos of my old home back in Germany and I will tell you a little more so that when you do go you will know what to expect. Many times you have seen the painting in our hallway of the old part of my German home village and the village church. Then there is the sketch hanging in the games room of our old family home in Germany. That was done by the mother of a student who stayed with us for a week some years ago. It was her way of saying "Thank you."'

I suggested it was perhaps time for Alex to join his grandmother. 'Otherwise your grandmother will think you don't love her any more.'

'Of course, I do, Granddad.'

Off we went, all three of us, with the dog leading the way.

'Well, Alex, if you come back one day next week before you go back to school again I will tell you what it was like when I was a little boy.'

'I will, Granddad.' He promised with a smile.

We were surprised to see Helene call so early in the morning. The mystery was quickly solved.

'Sorry can't stay, got to take Charlotte and her horse to a riding event at Tregembo.'

Tregembo is where Connie was working as a nursery maid for a year, just before we got married. Today it is an equestrian centre.

'Alex says he doesn't want to come and that he would rather stay here with you, as Granddad promised to tell him all about when he was a little boy.'

Helene went off, as always in a hurry. Alex came through the door, dressed in his oversized boxer shorts with shirt hanging out over them. He looked what he describes as 'Cool!' He was muttering 'Horses, horses, always horses.' He could not see much fun watching them in the drizzly rain.

'Well Alex it looks a good day for Granddad to tell you what it was like living in Germany when I was a boy.' We retreated into the sitting room – a very large room with two double French windows covering most of the south facing wall and overlooking the garden.

Our house is purpose-built, where the garden is one of the most prominent features and can be enjoyed all the year round, in all weathers. Wet or dry, summer or winter, only the minimum of effort is needed to maintain it. Much of the garden is lawn and to the left and right approximately thirty feet on either side are rising banks with a wide variety of shrubs and trees providing all-year-round colour – well over 150 different types. There is also a large neglected goldfish pond, with lilies, badly in need of attention. Having had two short spells in hospital and three weeks on a cruise, lack of time is given as a reason, when in reality it is just an excuse. Somehow, whenever I have felt the urge to do something big this year I have sat down until the urge has worn off. I am quite confident that all that should be done will be eventually achieved.

We made ourselves comfortable in front of one of these large windows. Here the story of my early life began to unfold. Alex had very little knowledge of my early days and he looked as if he was keen to hear all about it.

'I was born on 25th July 1925, the third child of Herr Josef and Frau Helene Mock. My first memory of my youth goes back to when I was still in my pram. My parents had gone to the funeral of a grandparent and I was left in the pram in the sitting room, in the care of a neighbour's wife. I recall clearly when I had been crying hysterically for some time when the neighbour's wife came with a bottle of milk. I can still see her with her hair done in a bun at the back of her head. Happiness was restored. My next event worth remembering was as darkness fell, my mother breastfeeding and cuddling me in the kitchen, beside the oven. When people say babies cannot remember anything, I disagree. Babies remember what they think extremely important at the time – like some adults! So the time until I was about three years old must have been pretty dull, until our shire horse stepped on my bare feet. You say, 'So what?' I invite you to try it and see if you remember.

'One hot June afternoon the following year, when suddenly the church bells rang, my father came in from the field with horse and wagon. He told me it meant a fire in the neighbouring village. Soon after, the horse-drawn pump appeared and Father joined them, all in a hurry. This was normal practice amongst the neighbouring villages. In this case, the burning barn could not be saved, but the fire was prevented from spreading to neighbouring buildings. In a hot continental summer afternoon, pumping water was hard work, and inflammation of my father's lungs developed as a result.

'My father had a weakness of the lung, a legacy of the First World War when he swallowed some gas on the Somme. He had two lengthy convalescence periods near Lake Geneva, but the weakness persisted. He never recovered and died on 30th June 1930. I greatly missed him especially when seeing other fathers playing with their children, my schoolmates, taking them to town or helping them to make bows and arrows. So I learnt at an early age to stand on my own two feet.

'I always remember my father as a kind man. On the evening after the funeral, mother, her sister, grandmother and aunties visited the grave. On the way home we children were playing around, when my grandmother said, 'They don't really know yet what happened.' Indeed we did not. Mother was left with five young children and a smallholding to run. Life was not easy for her. Her twin sister offered to take me and possibly adopt me. After a week it was clear that I would rather be home with my family.

'School in Germany started when you were six. As my birthday is on 25th July I did not qualify for the entry date at Easter so I needed a doctor's certificate to be made an exception. Maths, geography and history were my favourite subjects.

Music? – There was not a tune in me. I recall one occasion when I could not repeat a simple song, and the teacher hit me with his violin bow behind the ears. Silly devil! He must have damaged my hearing because he made it worse. In all fairness, a teacher with eight classes cannot have been ideal.

'Corporal punishment did not frighten everybody. On one occasion the school took great delight as a teacher administered six of the best on a backside – not mine – the child with his head between his legs. As it came to the fourth stroke, a sharp kick from the pupil, on the teacher's nose put a quick stop to the ceremony! The teacher had a shiner for a week. Complaining to the parents would have been counter-productive.

'I always felt my mother, probably under the influence of the local priest, was trying to guide me towards the church. The harder she tried the more I resented it. When I finally stated, 'I would rather be an apostle of the Devil than become a priest,' the speculation ended.

Alex listened very intently; a big boy for his age, with an enquiring mind, he was spellbound.

'Well, Alex, we did have to go to church every morning, at seven o'clock for mass. That was nearly compulsory. Then back home for a quick breakfast before going to school by eight.

'One day the normal routine was interrupted when a girl from my class shouted at the top of her voice, 'If I get married, I will marry the Mocks Schwarz – my nickname because of my dark hair. Can you imagine my embarrassment? If I could have emigrated that day at the age of eight, I would have done so.

'The school was only two or three hundred metres from home, above the fire station where the fire pumps and hoses were kept. You might say I was educated at a high school – one teacher and approximately thirty pupils from six to fourteen years old, one large room, the youngest pupil in the front, the older ones at the back. The total youth of the village in fact. Today you would find it difficult to imagine – no wonder the teacher sometimes lost his temper. He ruled with great respect. Or was it fear? He had a three-foot long cane and used it. We learned just the basics. School was from eight a.m. until one p.m., with plenty of time for homework.

'We all had little jobs to do at home. Mine was to bring in next day's firewood. It was all stored in the buildings around the farmyard. A large wooden box, next to the oven, with a lid on it and wide enough for two people to sit on, had to be filled. The biggest pieces at the bottom, some smaller ones near the top and twigs to light the fire the next morning at the very top.

'Any time left was spent in the orchard next to the house or in summer, in the small river marking the boundary. We spent hours diverting the water to get a stronger flow to drive our little water wheels. In winter there was always snow at sometime and we had great fun with our sledge, a four-seater to take all four of us, usually on a nice long stretch of the road coming down the hill. The river behind us usually froze over where the water was deeper and the flow very slow. The ice was strong enough to carry us. Where the water flow was faster the ice was thinner again. On one occasion, I came close to a fatal accident. I took a very good run to skate over it and ended up on the weaker ice, disappearing under the it. I eventually came out approximately fifteen feet down-river gasping for breath, my friends rescuing me. My mother came quickly to the scene and I have never seen her so worried or annoyed – before or since. The punishment was of the same quality and administered on the spot – never to be forgotten.

'The contour of the area around our village lends itself to skiing in winter. You can see the children at a very early age, flying down the hills as if they were born with skis on their feet. At sixteen I did a spectacular head over heels and landed myself in hospital for six weeks.

'On coming out of hospital the first thing I did was to sell the skis. I have never skied since.

'In summer and especially on Sunday afternoons we took every opportunity to roam around the woods on the east side of the village. The wood belonged to the Forestry Commission and the manager must have been young once himself. We had great fun building our tree-houses, no tree being too high or too difficult to get to the top; every boy laid claim to a tree of his own. Nobody was allowed to go anywhere near it. Whenever I go home I always visit my tree and see the initials RM still recognisable on the old beech.

'We made a lot of our amusement cutting our hazel sticks to make bows and arrows. There were no expensive toys or £1,000 computers for Christmas. An orange, plenty of home-grown apples, pears and nuts, a bar of chocolate, a few sweets and some home-baked biscuits covered with chocolate. It took very little to please children of those days.

'Since the 'thirties things have become better.'

Alex's eyes had seen something behind me. It was Grandma. 'Never mind,' she said. 'Our childhood was very similar. My mother was also a widow and had to go out to work.'

Alex has a lovely sense of humour and always gets good school reports. On the last one the remark at the bottom of his report was especially pleasing: 'His appointment as prefect has proved to be a very good choice.'

CHAPTER SEVENTEEN

A Paper on POWs

*T*oday it is hard for the present generation to understand that prisoner-of-war camps became a feature of the British landscape between 1942 and 1948. Eventually there were as many as 1,500 camps and hostels housing over 500,000 men.

In 1999, I came across a very interesting paper by Dr J Anthony Hellen on the legacy of Britain's prisoner-of-war camps. Here are some extracts from that paper:

'Some fifty years ago an extensive network of camps, hostels and hospitals across the United Kingdom, used for housing prisoner-of-war (POW) and surrendered enemy personnel (SEP) during and after the Second World War, was closed down. Many, and perhaps most, of the structures have since the summer of 1948 disappeared without visible trace or reverted to their original purpose, although at their peak some 390 major sites and – if main camps, satellites and hostels are included – 1500 camps were involved. Most of the 157,000 Italians and 402,000 Germans, in two overlapping phases, made up their transient populations. Towards the end of the war and thereafter some tens of thousands were billeted directly on farms. By contrast with Germany's network of 53 principal POW camps and 8 internment camps at 30 June 1944 in Europe, these camp settlements were eventually a locally well-known and widespread feature of normal civilian life across much of Britain, and they formed an important part of the cultural landscape although their overall extensiveness was deliberately kept from public awareness.

'However, unlike such enduring concrete fortifications as pillboxes and anti-tank obstacles, many POW camp structures built of timber or corrugated iron were sold at the end of the war and their sites have proved more prone to redevelopment, or neglect and decay, than these defensive structures.'

Later in his paper, Dr Hellen touched on some genuine British concern about fairness to the German POWs:

'Although the POW contribution was undeniably vital in the war years, in its aftermath it was eventually to raise considerable concern over the ethics and political expediency of prolonging compulsory labour as a *de facto* form of war reparations. The Bishop of Chichester argued that this response to a domestic manpower crisis employed Germans as "serf labour" on British farms (*cf* Lords debate on German POW and Internees, 12th February 1947, *Hansard*: col 561-608). Depending on their skilled or unskilled status, they were paid at an hourly rate of three-farthings to a penny-halfpenny or up to six shillings per forty-eight-hour week, at a time when the minimum wage for a labourer was seventy-five shillings a week.'

1 Above, Wechterswinkel, Germany ñ a nostalgic return in June 1996.

2 Below, Grandparents and grandchildren.

3 Bottom left, Grandson Alex with our dog Heidi.

4 Bottom right, Rudi and two acres of seedlings.

5 *Connie making music at home in 2000.*

6 *Poultry houses at Tremayne.*

7 *Retirement party at Land's End in 1990.*

8 *At an ostrich farm in Africa 1991.*

9 *Connie at the Great Wall of China.*

10 Opposite top, Granddaughter Charlotte on Mitch at Tregurtha, Cornwall. Her mother Helena is on the right.

11 Opposite, bottom, Our home Woodland Lodge at Praze-an-Beeble.

12 & 13 Above & below, In the garden at Woodland Lodge.

14 Opposite top, Rudi and Connie at a ranch in Uruguay in 1987.

15 Opposite bottom, Betty and Shirley packing flowers.

16 Above, The grandchildren

17 Below, A flower display in China.

18   *Rudi Mock and Son: just a small selection of different breeds of daffodil.*

And near the end of his paper, the author produces these interesting facts and figures:

'No less than 25,252 of the German POW 'elected to stay in Britain' after 1948, many of them remaining as farm-workers or marrying into farming families. In a news-letter to former German POW in Britain, dated May 1999, G Liebich has estimated that 25% of this number had since died, and a further 15% had emigrated to North America and Australia or returned to Germany by 1999.

'It is perhaps not generally known that whilst German POW were still widely employed in Britain, the British government was actively recruiting immigrant workers in Germany from October 1946 under the aegis of four programmes; operation 'Westward Ho' alone brought 74,412 workers to the country between April 1947 and December 1950.

Ironically, some were housed in former POW camps designated as hostels as they were vacated by fellow Germans.'

Of all the Germans staying over here, I know of only one who required British nationality: a friend of mine working as a postman in Manchester. It was a condition of employment. The view shared by the majority of us is that there is no compelling reason.

I regard myself as a European. European unity is for the benefit of us all. The coming down of the Berlin Wall was a wonderful thing. It was great news for Germany...East and West reunited and credit for this must go to Helmut Kohl, a great statesman…like a general winning an important battle without firing a shot.

'I was born a German and shall die a German. Connie has a dual nationality: British by birth and German by marriage, and she has a German passport. I pay my taxes the same as anybody else but I have no vote in British elections. That doesn't worry me. It's really an advantage because nobody can accuse me of voting or not voting for them…and I can criticise any of them. There's nothing sinister about this. I just feel it's right for me to live and die a German.

When I go back to Germany I find on the first couple of days I'm searching for German words and then after a day or two I'm back to normal. As for my English, I think with any language the earlier you start the better. I was a late starter in English and shall never have quite the command I would like. Then, of course, new words are introduced to a language and some words change their meaning. When I was a young man, the word 'gay' meant having a pleasant time. Now it's taken on such a meaning that a man I know who owned a cottage called 'Gay Cottage' felt it necessary to change the name!

CHAPTER EIGHTEEN

Reflections from Praze

People sometimes ask me, 'How would you do starting out again today?' They imply it would be more difficult but I don't agree. I certainly would not be afraid to start all over again if I were young again and knowing what I know now it wouldn't take me so long.

Somebody asked recently, 'If you had not been a flower-grower, what might you have done?'

Well, according to my mother, I'd have entered the church and may be one day have become a Roman Catholic priest but that was never a starter: probably something to do with the land or building. I have enjoyed restoring and creating properties. I've taken a great pride in doing a good job.

The repair and restoration of No 1 Bank Place at Falmouth was probably the most difficult building project for me. No doubt the people of Falmouth were very grateful when the scaffolding was finally removed after about ten years of holding up the derelict building. The Cornish Building Association showed their appreciation by awarding me a certificate of commendation.

A man, who has studied human behaviour, once said, 'Advice is what we ask for when we already know the answer but wish we didn't.'

There is something in that but if my grandchildren came to me asking advice about their future, I'd simply say this: 'Do whatever you want to do. Without it being *your* choice, you will always blame others for setbacks. That way if any glory is to be collected, it will also be *yours*.'

'The best thing I've done for the grandchildren is to give them a good private-school education. There's nothing snobbish about this. Private schools do two important things. They instil confidence and encourage the art of conversation.'

Looking back on my own career, I don't think I would have done anything very differently. From quite early on, I knew what I wanted and followed the light. I had confidence in myself and my ability. Not saying I never made a mistake. Show me a man who has never made a mistake and I'll show you a man who has never done anything either.

Making mistakes is a means of acquiring knowledge but, ideally, you learn from other people's mistakes. That's the least expensive way.

There was no grand plan in my life. I achieved my success step by step. I've always been a taker of opportunities. Tredrea was the beginning of my dream and sowing the seeds to fulfil my ambitions.

I have always liked working with flowers. In fact, for me, working with flowers is not work. It's been quite simply a labour of love and is probably all wrapped up with the fact that I'm a son of the soil. The soil must be in my genes. Flower-growing wasn't an original idea. When I worked with Mr Reeve, he grew anemones. In the late 1940s, a friend of a fellow prisoner-of-war had only half an acre of land but I could see that he produced a reasonable return and knew that if I had the land I could make a big success of it. Once I had the idea in my mind, I found out everything I could and questioned anyone I knew who had knowledge on the subject.

Fate brought me to the West Country. Here I discovered the Klondyke for flower-growing…a place where an investment of £100 can produce a return of 1,000 per cent…that's not counting labour. I was not a man working for somebody else, watching the clock. It was, as I say, a labour of love.

I soon discovered that daffodils can produce a high return, in flowers and bulbs, a double return. Had fate brought me to any other part of Britain, then I would almost certainly have returned to Germany when the war was over but here in West Cornwall I found myself in a beautiful place and I quickly recognised the possibility, even probability, of making good money through flowers.

If you look at the map on page 94, you will see that Area 40 is South-west Cornwall and the data about climate is proof of my reasoning. The Golden Square Mile for horticultural purposes is the area around Gulval, west of Penzance. The west-facing slopes of that coast make it almost frost-free, an advantage gradually lost as you move east. The growing period in Area 40 is 322 days, yet in the Gulval area it increases to almost 350 days. In East Cornwall this figure goes right down to only 294 days, in North-east England only 248 days.

I would not have contemplated any other agricultural or horticultural enterprise but growing flowers. A good living could be made for a small capital investment. West Cornwall was, in my opinion, the best place to do so, with our soft climate and good rainfall. It is recognised as the most suitable area for growing daffodils in the world. Not as storm-ravished as the Scilly Isles, there is more and cheaper land and economy of scale can be applied. It is also better in West Cornwall than the Channel Islands as our season begins two weeks earlier and our flower quality is better, especially the all-important length of stems – they even grow at night here!

Never was I attracted to livestock, especially cows. If you are a dairy farmer then you are tied to a cow's tail for seven days a week.

The land, on which I worked, was my college. On the land I watched others and asked questions. More than fifty years on,

I have the same thirst for knowledge. I didn't acquire my knowledge in a classroom. I did not go to professors. Instead I acquired my knowledge in the fields, working and watching. The key to all knowledge is asking questions of the right people. All these years later I'm still asking questions.

An expert in success in big business has said, 'There's always plenty of room at the top…room for action people.' And, of course, he's right. Certainly the success I've achieved has come not from just ideas but acting on those ideas…seeing it through.

The Rosewarne Horticultural Experiment Station was a fountain of information. Mrs Williams was a specialist with anything concerning anemones. Barbara Fry was the specialist concerning daffodils, her knowledge and devotion to her jobs was recognised world-wide and rewarded with an Award by the Queen. All the latest information was made freely available and updated. I made good use and greatly benefited from that advice on offer. It is generally acknowledged that the daffodil-breeding programme carried out by Barbara Fry at the experimental station was its greatest success and a huge benefit to the Cornish horticultural industry.

Life is rather like a ladder. The rung of a ladder was never meant to be a resting place but to hold a man's foot long enough to enable him to put his other foot higher.

I am not a practising Roman Catholic but I never deny the religion in my German upbringing.

To live a good Christian life does in my opinion not necessarily include going to church every Sunday. To do good deeds, or support good causes without advertising it is in my opinion a better way to practise Christianity. Wealth also demands responsibility.

You can do a lot of good outside the church but there is room for the parson or the priest in society as there are those who need spiritual guidance. Many people, especially older people, need reassurance. Personally, I don't believe in a hereafter. Though some of the chapels are closing down, I think the country chapels are closer to the people than the Roman Catholic Church.

There have been three turning points in my life: first, when I was taken prisoner on the Dutch-German border; then coming to Cornwall and, third, meeting Connie. I remember an uncle of mine emigrated to the United States and I secretly envied him. A smallholding was a difficult place from which to better yourself but I saw and recognised opportunities and went for them.

After the sale of business, there were lots of little things to do, selling bits and pieces. So it was a gradual winding down. With age, you move at a more leisurely pace. I take a keen interest in the Stock Exchange and read the *Financial Times* every Saturday. Connie is the main reader in our house.

It's true I have few hobbies. During my working life, there simply wasn't the time. Truth is, my work was my hobby. I didn't feel the need for diversions. Growing flowers was a creative way of life but I can understand that someone doing repetitive work in a factory day after day does need the stimulus of holidays and change. My dreams and my ambitions have been fulfilled – with more to spare.

I've never had the desire to live anywhere other than Cornwall. It's a big holiday destination. Connie and I both think Cornwall is as attractive as anywhere else in the world. Oh, that it had a better more reliable summer!

Despite that, I believe the holiday industry will continue to prosper and farmers' wives, with their bed and breakfast and evening meals, will bring in extra income.

Connie and I did not look beyond Praze for our retirement home. We have built the house of our choice and laid out the garden the way we like it. Where would we find a better place? And we are so close to the rest of the family. We are financially secure and we have given the children a leg-up and I believe we are giving the grandchildren the best possible start in life.

Money has not really changed me. OK, we are able to holiday abroad and enjoy a few luxuries but those are the perks. We lead a comparatively simple life. I do the cooking on Sunday. That means we go out for a good Sunday lunch and it takes care of the washing up. I'm a very contented man.

There is no other place on earth we would rather live.

Where else in the world would we find a place where you are greeted by the dawn chorus at five o'clock in the morning and lulled back to sleep again by the twittering, singing, whistling and whatever these little birds do? I can look over the flower boxes on the veranda down into the garden, to check what progress the flowering shrubs have made since yesterday morning. I can look out over the open countryside, for miles, and on the horizon is an old chimney stack, a reminder of the Cornish mining history. I can watch a bunny-rabbit having his breakfast on the lawn; see the first rays of the rising sun reflecting on the shining leaves of a beech tree, creating a hundred different shades of green. I can come down in the morning and find a squirrel outside the French window, waiting patiently for his first feed of the day. Where else can we find a spot like this?

With our family living close by, that's where we built our dream house, with more than an acre of garden, laid out the way we like it, planted with shrubs and trees of our choosing. Gardens are to be enjoyed by their owners. Ours is now maturing, but I am not a slave to it. A leisurely drive for an hour and a half on a ride-on mower takes care of the lawn once a week. Spraying twice a year with a weedkiller deals with the weeds. Life is good to us. As the saying goes, 'Enough is as good as a feast.' Enough for the rest of our lives gives a comfortable feeling and security. We are happy here and content.

CHAPTER NINETEEN

❧

Journeys of a Lifetime

*T*ravel?

Some may ask, 'What has travel to do with the Rudi Mock story?'

'Well, quite a lot!' is the answer. Our dream was not to make money and pile it high.

The writer Robert Louis Stevenson said, 'To travel hopefully is a better thing than to arrive.' Frankly I think Mr Stevenson was talking through his literary hat.

Connie and I have planned some memorable destinations and we have rarely been disappointed.

A while back someone enquired, 'What do you hope to do when you have sold your business?'

Our answer was quite simple: 'To make life easier for ourselves and our family...and to travel.' By 1987 our objectives were within our reach – we had surpassed them and had come to a point where we could fulfil our dreams.

Even Hitler realised that all work and no play makes Jack a dull boy. He introduced compulsory holidays and cheap holidays for the workers with the 'Kraft durch Freude' programme, Strength through Enjoyment. If you do repetitive work, a break is a must. If your job is creative, you can delay it.

Some years – some events – stand out vividly in the memory. Hungary in 1956 was such a European chapter when Russian reinforcements were sent into the country to quell an uprising that threatened to take Hungary out of the Eastern Bloc. The streets of Budapest echoed to the sound of gunfire as freedom fighters faced Soviet armoured divisions. As I watched television film that year and read about the tragic events in our newspapers – 4,000 Hungarians died and 200,000 more fled to the West – little did I realise that I would be there one day as a visitor.

Our ambition to travel and see the world was, at first, farming orientated, mostly with other farmers, 'men only'. My first was a visit to the state-owned poultry-breeding farm in Babolna, Hungary. It had many other interests as well, pigs and sheep breeding plus 205 Arabian horses; seven hundred and fifty-one mares, bred from English thoroughbreds. The noble Arabian horses have been bred here for nearly two centuries and they are among the most beautiful and intelligent in the equine world. There is almost a poetry about their movements – and the horse-drawn carriages take you back to another world when horses provided the power in transport.

They have 4,225 employees, of which 160 were university-trained and 260 with high-school background. The modern Babolna was built up according to the latest techniques of animal production and husbandry. We were made very welcome at the highest level, shown films of their breeding programme, inspected their hatchery, test farm and the 'Tetra' parent stock. Dinner was in the farm restaurant and it was interesting to see the directors and workers eating together. We stayed at the farm hostel for the night. Breakfast was somewhat different: my stomach surprised to be greeted with a double brandy first thing in the morning, instead of the customary cup of warm water at home in Cornwall. After watching a fine display by their famous Arab horses we said our goodbyes, well satisfied with our visit; our minds broadened, we returned to Budapest and more sightseeing – and then home again.

When I returned home from one of these trips, a local man said to me: 'What a waste of time and money…'

But I disagreed: 'I always come home feeling it was money well spent,' I explained. 'You meet new friends, usually forward-looking people, successful in their chosen fields. You have an exchange of opinions and often that reassures you about your next expansion in the pipeline.'

When we booked our first cruise on the *Canberra* before it was requisitioned to carry troops to the Falklands, our travel agent offered us an alternative to visit the same places, but on a Russian boat. After long deliberations, it was considered the best alternative and I pointed out that at least we could be sure it would not be requisitioned again. The ship was all right, and so was the food, perhaps not quite so fanciful as some other boats. One day we shared a dinner table with a family from Birmingham who were not satisfied with the menu. They complained that it never had baked beans on it. This got the chef in a spin. He was anxious to please. He could help with about a dozen varieties of beans, but he had never actually baked the beans. I don't know if that family every got the dream meal of their life, but it takes all sorts – and different tastes.

This boat had also a casino, in common with all other boats. But there was an important difference: on the wall behind the table was a plaque saying, 'Do not bet more than you can afford to lose. The tables are set against you.'

Very good advice, and it was not in small print either.

Later, on a tour of South Africa, along the garden route, we passed through a small independent state, where gambling was allowed. Most of our group paid a visit to the hotel casino with an agreed limit of £50 in their pockets. Connie said it was not for her and left.

I stayed and watched with interest and that plaque on the wall in the casino on the Russian boat stayed firmly in my mind. A few card games warmed everybody up. I watched one of the two tables and it was win one, lose one. The table was joined by one person, winning more often than losing. A member of the casino, discreetly appeared and recorded every bet he placed and some of the players followed him, as he was more often successful than they were. This went on for some time. No large sums were placed. Eventually, another member of the casino joined to observe. It appeared the players had a slight advantage in winning numbers, disregarding not knowing the actual value of the bets or guessing. The table was soon closed. After some time, what appeared to be the most successful punter was playing one-to-one with a member of the casino in a corner, well screened from the public.

By the time I had left, all the others from our group had long gone. Connie told me they had been back some time and were in the bar, probably to forget. Connie asked what it was like. I reminded her of that plaque on the wall in the casino of the Russian ship: sound advice and it saved me fifty quid.

China

Back in the 1200s when the explorer and merchant Marco Polo returned to Venice from China, he claimed that he had discovered a land richer and more sophisticated than his own. Few people believed him but he was telling the truth. The Chinese civilisation is one of the oldest in the whole world – by about 1700 BC the Shand Dynasty already had a society which worked bronze, understood the craft of writing and had a number of large towns.

A visit to China is one of the world's unique travel experiences. This vast mysterious country is full of exotic sights and sounds. China remains a country steeped in mystique and fascination. This time Connie came as well.

Our tour was again a farming plus sightseeing journey, organised by the feed firm Dalgety. We started with a flight to Peking (Beijing). On our arrival we were met by the local tour guide and the national guide – an honour not many tours were granted. When we booked into our hotel, we were overwhelmed by its five-star quality: a joint American/Chinese venture. Peking has a wealth of attractions, like the Imperial Palace, Tiananmen Square – the largest public square in the world, the Temple of Heaven – a masterpiece of geometric fifteenth-century architecture, the majestic Summer Palace and much more.

The farming in that area is on the 'People's Commune' system: one man per six cows. Not to reveal the cow's origin, they called them 'Peking black and whites', in other words 'Friesians'. In the evening we enjoyed a Peking Duck Banquet. Have you ever eaten with chopsticks? Sounds frightening – I had packed a knife and fork and carried them in my pocket. When I saw Connie nearly succeeding with her first attempt I could see that with a little practice it was not so difficult. Chinese food is excellent. The tables are round, and for eight or nine people, with another turntable about four inches higher; all dishes are placed on this inner table and everyone helps themselves. There are at least two fish dishes, two meat, then two poultry, for a start, with more dishes frequently removed and replaced with even more appetising ones. This goes on until finally soup arrives. That is the last dish. The very small soup spoons reminded me of grandfather's curved pipe. I have always heard that Chinese cooking is amongst the best. I agree. I would not guarantee that this would apply to all restaurants, but it was certainly so in this joint-venture five-star hotel!

A visit to a strange country can sometimes be a cultural shock. Our visit to China was such an experience. Their ideals are, in some ways, very alien to first-time visitors from the west.

The state already has all you ever had. All your needs are satisfied on a communal basis. All land belongs to the state. When we were there, the state had started giving sufficient land to individuals or families to build their own homes – and some communes had begun to provide comfortable places for the elderly.

Much of the land is farmed by individuals on the clear understanding that an agreed quantity is sold to the state at low prices. The rest is sold on the open market where supply and demand are the price regulators – as in the west – but this is only on a small scale.

The time of the little red book had already passed.

In Peking, our assistant guide told me, 'When I was a student, we all went into the fields working for the common good, waving our little red books and catching our quota of flies…but our enthusiasm gradually faded away.'

We could see no birds in this vast country.

One explanation is they have eaten them all. Another is because there are no flies, there are no birds.

We were told, 'All Chinese people are equal and therefore get equal pay.'

Our national guide, who had been the Chinese representative for tourism in Australia, explained, 'I earn the equal of twenty-five American dollars per month.'

The official Chinese explanation is: 'We provided you with an education out of community funds. Therefore the community is entitled to the benefit of your service or services.'

I asked him, 'Why don't you emigrate to a country where you can earn more?'

'Emigration is not allowed,' was his simple reply.

There are many statues in China symbolising the unity of all – and equals pulling together for the common good. Chairman Mao is lying in state, overlooking the square. He looked peaceful enough. I do not know what will happen if the millions of Chinese people develop a taste for our western goods – and find a way to pay for them.

In China there is a degree of religious freedom.

On our flight home, I sat next to an American missionary who had been in China for a dozen years. He told me, 'We missionaries must not go out into society to canvas or convert but the Chinese people themselves are free to come to our churches voluntarily. They must make the first move.'

Next to Xian, which has an 8,000-year history and was the largest city in the world. One of the greatest historical discoveries in China was made there in 1974, when peasants digging a well unearthed thousands of life-sized terracotta figures guarding the main entrance to the tomb of Qin Shi Huangdi. It is estimated that some 6,000 figures are buried there. We also visited the Great Wall of China. One afternoon, we visited a small-scale farming operation; you invariably drew comparisons with the large-scale commune system. The Nanjing area is well known for its large-scale agricultural communes growing grain, tea, vegetables, fruit and melons. The experimental farm was of great interest, especially the cross-fertilisation with wheat, to test the resistance to diseases. Our train journey to Wuxi was a new experience: armchairs in the waiting room, an exceptional train service with green tea served free of charge; a good view of the countryside and the progress being made in the agricultural fields.

We saw the mystery of acupuncture in practice: approximately thirty people in a room lying on beds, with trousers rolled up above the knees, needles about four-inches long sticking everywhere facing in any direction and one nurse attending to all. She appeared very experienced in placing the needles. If I were playing darts in the pub, I would prefer to have her on my side rather than playing for the opposition.

I discovered there is an interesting link between the Chinese landscape and acupuncture. The Chinese consider the whole landscape, both fields and the mountains, as one giant creature

– the lung-mei lines are similar to the lines in acupuncture. In each case, the aim is to focus and harness the energies carried by the respective lines of energy.

In Britain, ley lines are essentially twentieth-century thinking but in China they have been recognised for hundreds of years.

From Wuxi, we visited an agricultural commune to see how it works. Each commune has fifteen brigades, and each brigade has fifteen teams. Throughout China, it is known for its high productivity. We took lunch with them. The agricultural practice in China is still in a mechanical sense, back in the Middle Ages. A three-foot wide combine harvester looked more like a toy a prosperous farmer over here would buy for his children for Christmas. A lot of the grain harvest on the smaller places is done with a sickle and then put on a road for the lorries to drive over and thrash it – all very primitive. We did not see any use of modern fertiliser but all the agricultural and human waste is collected and put to use.

Family life consists normally of grandparents, and grandchildren sleeping in one bed the size of a small room, and heated in winter. The young wife usually is helping the grandmother in that order. All land is owned by the state, but now the individual can own enough ground to build himself a house. They have great respect for their parents, and look on it as an honour to make them comfortable. In one commune we saw what would appear, by Chinese standards, luxury old people's homes. But China is on the change, and we are glad that we visited it before its modernisation.

The next day we took a leisurely cruise to Hangzhou. The lake was rich with fish. Picturesque West Lake, with its gardens, temples, tea-houses, make it a town so typically Chinese. Our tour leader allocated the rooms every day so everybody had the best sometime. West Lake was our lucky day. The hotel was at times used for top party and other important meetings by the highest in the land. The large veranda had the flagpole on it, which indicated that our suite was the very best of the best.

The furniture was in solid mahogany, deep armchairs, and a bathroom to match, colour TV as well. The bedroom was of the same quality. Connie put all her worn clothes in a plastic bag hidden in the back of the wardrobe. You would have thought it was safe, but much to our surprise on our return in the evening, everything was washed, beautifully ironed and on the shelves in the wardrobe. Who says everything Communist is bad? The view from our suite was breathtaking.

We visited the renowned Longjing Tea Plantation (Dragon Well Tea). It is harvested three times a year and the leaves are processed by hand with great care preserving the quality of the leaves and flavour, we toured farms and had meetings with the managers and workers. The distances in China can be considerable so we took to the air to Guilin, where we spent the day cruising on the River Lik, through lush land, ducks and geese on the river banks, water buffalo feeding in the river, and other buffalo pulling the plough. A Chinese poet of the seventh century AD described the area around Guilin thus: 'The river forms a green belt, the mountains are like hairpins.' In fact the image most westerners have of China is actually the landscape of Guilin. The lush green plains, the picturesque river, the lakes and pools and the muted tones of towering rock formations have been celebrated in Chinese poetry and art for centuries. Our cruise was like a journey through a living Chinese painting. Whenever Connie and I talk about our Chinese holiday, the boat trip on the River Lik always comes into it.

Our visit to the Great Wall of China was breathtaking. It is the only man-made object visible from outer space: most impressive. Even with all our modern machinery today it would be a major undertaking in any century.

Right from the start of our tour, we were very impressed with the healthy appearance and cleanliness of all people. Nearly all were dressed in white shirts, and dark trousers, and very polite. We were entertained most evenings by high-class gymnastics, or other displays, also banquets by heads of an area and the inevitable endless toasts. We were well attended to and great efforts were made to make our journey enjoyable. Another lasting memory is the strategically placed slit in the trousers of the boys – makes for inventive efficiency.

A little Chinese dress we brought back for our granddaughter made her parentage questionable, with her dark hair and tan.

Our flight to Canton brought us to the most western city in China and the one with the most western influences. On the way to breakfast, we remarked that the ducks were up early until we discovered it was a tape recording. In the breakfast room, the waiters were on strike, and those in charge had to hand out the cutlery and the rest was self-service. It was very much in contrast to the rest of our tour, where the staff were hand-picked, smart, impeccably polite and helpful.

We went by train to Hong Kong and back to the western world. In China, people were absolutely honest, when one of our members left his camera behind, the chief of the village travelled fifteen miles to return it. In Hong Kong, a man with a rifle between his legs sat in a corner of a jewellery shop just as a warning. You can get a suit made to measure in thirty hours, silk ties ten per cent of the price in England, high class oil paintings 25" x 36", take your pick from a two-foot pile at £4.50 each. All hotels are air-conditioned, but as soon as you open the front door you step out into an oven.

Our holiday to China was from 8th-27th May. Climate-wise it was just right. The winters are cold, the summer hot. We shall always remember our holiday in 1986 to China as one of our best – before it changed.

The Chinese are very superstitious. They firmly believe that the sky is full of evil spirits to bring bad things upon us. That is why many of their roofs have a turn upwards again, so that when these evil spirits come down to do us harm, the roofs direct them back up again at speed.

Israel

Born in conflict, the modern state of Israel has had a history of war with its strong, determined Arab neighbours – many times its size.

The return of Jews in 1948 to their historic land ended eighteen centuries of exile. Today there is real pride in the achievements of this tiny state surviving against enormous odds.

Israelis are very proud of their reputation for innovation and staying one step ahead of their competitors. Today that means growing high-quality fresh produce – and packing and delivering it to the customer in the best possible state. Much of the farming is done not necessarily on the communally run kibbutz, which now appear to be in decline (some are even converting to industrial enterprises), but by private farmers who live in 'Moshavs' – settlements, where they co-operate for common services, yet run their own businesses. We have seen a large cow herd on a five-acre holding (which is, I believe, the maximum size permissible), with all the rest of the feeding stuff brought in from the settlement.

Water is probably the most restricting factor to farming in Israel. That is probably the reason why Israel is leading in irrigation techniques and drip-feeding. Labour is also a problem. Working on a kibbutz, or anywhere else, is no longer an attraction for students from the western world. The Far East is now a bigger supplier on a two-year basis, from countries like Thailand or Slovakia from Eastern Europe. We visited a large vegetable farm near the sea of Galilee, owned by an Israeli, but all workers were Palestinians. The high input from highly educated members was evident on most farms. Most were educated in America, and surprisingly Germany.

A study tour in Israel can be very productive, as you spend

very little time on the road. The holy places are, of course, of special interest. The way of life has changed very little for the Arabs. Outside Nazareth, we saw a gang of women cultivating the ground, the same way as 2,000 years ago, while the men were in town drinking coffee. We asked our guide for an explanation. His reply was, 'We put that question to many women. The reply is always the same. "My husband happy, we both happy." This is one thing the men have got right!' When staying in a kibbutz on the north side of the Sea of Galilee, we visited the Golan Heights and the troops on the border. All were very relaxed, like all the military in Israel. At the source of the River Jordan we saw how grain was ground 2,000 years ago. One of the most interesting places was the Dead Sea. It was at the end of a long hot summer and the water was full with minerals. One of our members was sitting in the water catching up on the news by reading the daily paper. If you want to stand still you would have to keep your balance by moving your hands lightly or your legs move on while your body stays – a new experience. Two hours in there and a good shower afterwards and you feel like a born-again Christian.

Israel is a very small country, full of history and we can learn a lot from them. On our journey along the coast, we saw a tanker out at sea at the end of the oil pipeline from the Arab countries. We enquired, 'What happened to his pipeline when all these wars were going on?' He assured us that this oil never stopped flowing. After a little pause he added, 'War is one thing, business is another.' We spent two days in Jerusalem where we met the farm minister, amongst others. A visit to the Wailing Wall on a Friday night was proof of how religion plays a large role in the life of Israel. On Saturday morning, market day for the Arabs, just outside the city wall, is also the meeting place for most men, like it was in the days of Christ. There may be a donkey or two, a few sheep and poultry. Some came on donkeys. We also saw two Land Rovers. The dowry of an eligible daughter may also be an important point for some discussions.

The road to Calvary may be one of great spiritual significance but today it is a trade route, full of selling points. For these people, selling almost anything you can possibly think of, it is a bit like Tintagel, back in Cornwall, which has turned a famous story into a business venture.

The better Arab shops have a prosperous look and I asked one shopkeeper: 'What do you think of the occupation of Jerusalem by the Israelis?' He was, of course, exempt from taxes regarding 'defence'.

From his considered reply, you might have thought he was something of a politician. 'I cannot answer but you can.... How would you like to be occupied by the Germans?'

It was an interesting example of answering a question with another question and, of course, he did not know my German background.

I feel I could write a book about Jerusalem – and I recommend it as a worthwhile destination.

South American Odyssey

Our tour started with a boat ride around Miami Beach, where the rich and famous live, some on the man-made islands, with security guards at their gates. Next, to Brazil, a vast country of natural beauty, astonishing vistas and unforgettable ambience, where surprise after surprise awaits you. In the south, the characteristics and climate are often compared to Europe. In the south-west is Latin America's industrial and cultural centre. To the mid-west are its twenty-one Wetlands, with wildlife reserves to the north-east, where miles and miles of white beaches offer total relaxation and to the north is the amazing Amazon region, the largest forest reservation in the world.

As the old song runs, 'There is an awful lot of coffee in Brazil.' Curiously though, Brazil has riches beyond wild dreams yet very little money. Nevertheless, it is a fun-loving, football-crazy and car-mad society. Their greatest footballer, Pele, has become a kind of folklore figure in the history of the game.

Distances stretch in this vast land. It runs 2,683 miles from north to south and rather more from east to west and it has a coastline of 4,595 miles.

We enjoyed Brazilian hospitality, cuisine – and paradise. Deep in the Amazon jungle, twelve miles upstream, is the confluence of the Amazon and the Rio Negro. The jungle was a new experience. So was a visit to an Indian reservation, a peaceful community, not knowing anything about the bestiality of the other world. Brasilia is the new purpose-built capital of Brazil – flat, rising ground around man-made lakes, with over two million people. It was designed by Oskar Niemeir of Germany. As his wife was killed in a road accident, there are wide open spaces, but no road crossings. Rio is the highlight of any visit to Brazil. We had some vivid, beautiful memories: a visit up to the Sugarloaf Mountain, by cable car, with superb views over the town and Copacabana Beach; a Brazilian-style barbecue and a Samba and carnival show in the evening – the costumes alone cost half a million pounds. The hall, holding about 20,000 people, was packed: a breathtaking show, never to be forgotten. Afterwards, it was followed by a sing-song from most of the approximately twenty different nationalities present, with their favourites. Everybody joined in as if they knew them all. It was a marvellous atmosphere. After the barbecue, the stomach was a little rebellious. Next day, we went by cog railway to the 'Christ the Redeemer' statue; 2,400 feet up, the statue is 120 feet high, weighing 1,200 tonnes. We had a glorious view of the town and the harbour of Rio. The way up was lined with a splendid collection of trees from Central America, India and local shrubs – a spectacular sight. The way down was by road, past the waterfall, seafront and shopping centre. No wonder everybody wants to live in Rio. That was the main reason why the government decided to move the capital, Brasilia, inland, to encourage development there and discourage further concentration around Rio. The next day we went to Iguacu, the famous waterfalls, about which Mrs Eleanor Roosevelt said, '...these spectacular falls make Niagara look like a kitchen faucet.'

We paid a short visit to Paraguay and saw the biggest dam in the world on Paranta River. Work was still in progress, costing sixteen billion dollars, with an output equal to ten atomic power stations, it is a joint venture with Brazil.

After gaining independence from Spain, early in the nineteenth century, Paraguay quickly became an important power in South America. But in the mid-1860s up until 1870, the country lost three-quarters of its million-plus population in bloody conflict against the combined forces of Argentina, Brazil and Uruguay.

Then we went on to Uruguay, one of the continent's smallest nations which was once considered 'the Switzerland of South America' because of its combination of prosperity and neutrality. For the greater part of the last century, Uruguay has had a democratic government, a good welfare state and a high standard of lifestyle.

Prosperity was due to the rich terrain and the mild climate. As much as ninety per cent of the land is suitable for agriculture but only something less than ten per cent is cultivated. The rest of the rolling landscape is grazed by huge herds of cattle and flocks of sheep.

Montevideo is a premier seaside resort and our stay coincided with the visit of the French President, staying in the French Embassy. But all other hangers-on stayed in our hotel: security everywhere. The staff were very efficient in serving our meal.

We found out later that this was the night they chose the Miss Uruguay. Soon the sugar daddies with their handlebar moustaches arrived, with dolly birds on their arms, young enough to be their granddaughters.

Argentina was our next destination. Buenos Aires is a large city with many Europeans, the population is thirty per cent Spanish, forty per cent Italian, twenty per cent German/French/English.

The majority of Argentines think of themselves as quite different from other South American people. They have a high opinion of themselves: considering themselves more sophisticated and better educated.

There is a strong European influence and the capital city of Buenos Aires – where one-third of the population lives – has the air of a European city. This is not surprising when you learn that most of the people here are descended from European immigrants and there is a sizeable British community in the city – resulting from the times when the British came here to build the railways.

There are very good old buildings of character, a nice park, open spaces, the 'Square of the Lost Children' where mothers meet every Thursday at three p.m. to remember their missing sons and daughters. A war memorial has the inscription 'It is not over yet'. Our guide pointed out the Ministry of Defence and said, 'This is the factory for old presidents.' There are many symbols of the early settlers. There are good West-End type shops too, and quality at half the price.

One evening we shared a table for dinner with two ladies from London – one a middle-aged widow. Her children were grown up and left home and the other, with the appearance of a modern-day business lady –tall, flaxen-haired, good-looking and with an air of self-assurance to match. She looked a well-preserved fifty-year-old, but must have been at least sixty or she would not have qualified to travel with Saga at the time. They told us of their exploits that afternoon. Both had come with an empty suitcase and had been taking advantage of the extremely low shop prices. Given the shopping that they were talking about, they must have saved a large part of their holiday cost. Connie had bought a leather skirt in Uruguay and I had a made-to-measure leather jacket. We thought we had done quite well. After a good meal and glass of wine, we just sat and had some light-hearted talk with the two of them. They were friends and met once a week for a meal and perhaps a show on a regular basis. Joan, the tall one, was an estate agent, dealing in high-quality property in London and she was telling us about some funny experiences she had with some clients. Some were just agents, shortlisting properties for people to inspect. One kept viewing again and again until she realised it was not the property he was after but a date with her. We expressed surprise that an attractive woman like her, who could still turn a man's head at sixty years, was still unattached and put claim to her virginal purity in a light-hearted way. When we expressed surprise, with an expression of blissful happiness on her face she eventually said, 'Ah...' Gwen, her friend, was waiting to hear whatever was to follow. Had she discovered the secret of eternal youth? No, it was much simpler than that. The sentence started with 'Ah...' concluded with, 'I have been to the invisible menders a few times. It is surprising what modern surgery can do.' Had Princess Grace had the knowledge of that London estate agent she would not have needed to worry before she married her prince.

But on the minus side there were power cuts for some time on most days: a city with history and proud of it, but down on its knees. In the South of Argentina is Bareloche, an area very much like a European winter sports resort, known as 'Little Switzerland', with similar houses and landscape. Lakes are connected to each other and many Germans have settled here.

Our odyssey included Chile. Like the backbone of a large animal, Chile runs its long, thin course down the continent's broad back. It has an incredible range of climate: from deserts to steaming forests, to icy wastes.

The country is very agricultural in many parts and the scenery reminded me of Devon forty years ago. The capital, Santiago, appeared prosperous with large crowds at the races on a Sunday evening. We passed large workers' estates and there are many Indians fighting to survive on a very small piece of land, living in very primitive shelters. The journey to Chile took us over the 'Great Divide' in the Andes, where suddenly all rivers were flowing west instead of eastwards.

In Bolivia, we came to the capital, La Paz, which is 12,000 feet high, the highest capital city in the world. On arriving at the airport, many people were affected by the high altitude and were a little light-headed. A cup of 'caca' – a cup of tea with a little cocaine – soon put that right. It did not make me become addicted!

We soon discovered that poverty is rife in many South American countries but nowhere is it worse than in this landlocked nation. Despite the fact that Bolivia has extensive mineral resources, the country and its inhabitants remain among the poorest in Latin America. This is the result of history: two wars and political instability since winning independence in 1825. They have had as many as 190 governments in 150 years!

The courting habits are unique in Bolivia. All women wear Derby hats. If they are placed on the right, they are married. If on the left, they are unmarried. These hats are always worn at the many religious festivals. The young men study the local talent and if a girl takes his fancy – he will pinch her hat and run. If the girl responds by chasing him, it is not the hat she wants to retrieve. If they want to live together, he will have to speak to his father first. She then takes him home to her family and they will live together for eighteen months. In most cases, a big Catholic wedding will follow. If however they decide marriage is not for them, the man will leave. If there is a child – then the child will stay with the mother and any further husband would take over responsibility for both – and the marriages are usually very stable.

The biggest highlights were a trip on the Lake Titicaca, and meeting the men who built the reed boats for the Polynesian expedition, and a visit to the Moon City, a large area where nature has reduced the clay to figures of all shapes and sizes: an eerie place and feeling. Another interesting thing is the women wear as many as seven skirts at a time. Why and in which order they change them we could not find out. Maybe they just want to make it interesting for their men?

We went past a big airbase, used by the Americans to stop the drug trade. The dealers just left and came right back again. Forty kilos of cocoa leaf makes one kilo of cocaine, which, in turn, makes 200 dollars. While the average wage is fifty dollars a month, this trade will not stop – until more rewarding alternative employment can be found.

So on to Peru. Lima, ancient capital of Peru, is known as the 'City of Kings'. The Gold Museum is massive with very high security – all sorts of armoury, statues and anything you can think of made from gold, 18,000 pieces. Lima resembles a South European city: Cuzco is the ancient capital of the Inca civilisation and the ruins of Sacasayhuamon. A four-hour narrow-gauge train journey took us through the Sacred Valley of the Incas, and up into the mountains to the base of Machu Pizchu, claimed to be the eighth wonder of the world. To look from the railway station at the vertical wall, with the buses looking like Dinky toys, crawling up is a fantastic sight. A bus took us to the summit, and a tour of the Inca fortress. When we reached the top, I told Connie that this journey converts more unbelievers to faith than most parsons could claim in a lifetime's work. She replied, 'We have the way down yet to come.' These Inca ruins were unique, the full history and mystery, why they were built, and how, remain unanswered questions.

Sadly, the Peru of today is scarred by poverty and violence. Many of the people are the victims of an unequal social structure and they have a desperate struggle to survive in their shanty towns.

Our next destination was Quito, the capital of Ecuador. Close by you can stand with one leg in the southern hemisphere and the other in the northern hemisphere.

The political scene in this country is almost as wild as its landscape. There are more than thirty active volcanoes and, like the eruptions in the mountains, there is a history of rumbling power struggles. You could almost say there are three Ecuadors: the west, the central mountainous areas of the Andes and the east. Each of these three areas has its own climate, customs and attitudes.

Many women work as shepherds in the Andes of Ecuador, children carried on the backs of their mothers – and cocoa leaves – a source of cocaine – are often chewed to combat tiredness at the high altitudes.

The hotel manager assured us that the water was perfectly suitable to drink, but advised us to stick to bottled water or we might end up with the dreaded 'Inca quickstep'. This applied to all South American countries.

After the evening meal, the coffee is usually taken in the lounge and social chat with others. On most tours, there is normally one person who stands out and leaves a deep impression. This evening we were joined by a Scottish lady and another lady who obviously had class. She was certainly aware of her own importance and was used to being looked after by others – with luggage to match. She was of average build, well preserved, blue-rinsed (of course) with wrinkles but not too many that a good ironing could not have improved. Her eyelashes were, at a conservative guess, approximately three inches long. Her accent was of somebody who appeared to have learnt English in later life. She immediately reminded me of Zsa Zsa Gabor. She looked the part, with the accent to match. I don't know why, but that's the best way I can describe her. Her husband was dead, and she came from Hungary, and while the war was on her husband had been Minister of Information there, an equivalent to the job Dr Goebbels held in Germany.

She told us how towards the end of the war, trying to escape from the advancing Russians to North Germany, life was difficult, rations short. Farmers hoarding food was a crime that carried a death sentence. The Scottish lady had some difficulty in understanding her speech, but her ears were pricked. 'Zsa Zsa Gabor' obviously did not leave Hungary with the pockets empty, so they had valuables to barter with the local farmers. Intelligent people are not always the most practical and the way they slaughtered the pig and shaved the bristles off with her husband's razor had us in stitches. We laughed uncontrollably, with tears running down our faces. The kidneys, heart and liver they did not know what to do with and did not think they were edible. They buried them. With rations below life-support level, you can imagine how their friends felt the next day when they found out. They were quickly dug up again. The whole performance of slaughtering and cutting up this pig was quite a story. In the end, she joined in the laughter. This was the most all four of us have ever laughed in our lives. If the real Zsa Zsa Gabor could tell her life story like this woman, I can quite see why she had so many husbands. They probably died laughing. But there would always be others waiting to be entertained again.

We visited all South American countries with the exception of Columbia, have seen the most interesting scenery of the continent, stayed in the best hotels and enjoyed the best food they had to offer. We have met many interesting people and made good friends. It was an odyssey we shall always treasure.

We were on our way home to Miami when we learned the stock market had collapsed and the 1987 hurricane had crossed Southern England, but not over our area. There was no need to worry about the stock market. Our values were in property, daffodils, plant and machinery. Why do people have to ring the first time they see a phone after five weeks? It was nice to come home and find everything was fine. Andrew had managed well without us. Our 'wanderlust' was well satisfied – for the time anyway.

The Nile and Egypt

In Egypt, you wonder about the very nature of time.

The facts are these: Ancient kingdom of the Pharaohs, Egypt is the location of one of the oldest civilisations in the world. There is a recorded history stretching back 5,000 years.

There is, though, another side of the Egyptian life – there are modern wonders such as the High Dam at Aswan on the Nile. Egypt, of course, is a kind of doorway between Africa and Asia. With its access to the Mediterranean and the Red Sea, it has always been a tempting prize and possibility for invaders.

The Nile is the longest river in the world, at 4,160 miles long. Egypt is as dependent on the Nile now as it was in the days of the Pharaohs, a land of great contrasts, ancient and modern, rich and poor. Famous for the lush Nile Valley and the huge monuments of the past, ninety-six per cent of the population live in the delta and the twelve-mile-wide strip along the river. Witness the moving of the temple of Pharaoh Rameses II at Abu Simble to a higher site above the flood level of the Lake Nasser. Camels are widely used. The Suez Canal remains the country's biggest earner, with 17,500 ships using it. The Great Pyramid Khutu, built about 2590BC is one of the seven wonders of the ancient world. The Sphinx, a mythical beast with a man's head and lion's body, symbolised the Pharaoh Kafafre's son. From Luxor and Kornak, we visited numerous temples and burial grounds, including the Valley of the Tombs of the Kings. The intense heat, even in November, made it necessary to be there at six o'clock in the morning to avoid queuing up as well. The Valley of the Queens is less secretive and not quite so hot. Cairo is also rich in mosques and museums. Bargaining is necessary and you will always be pestered for 'baksheesh' (alms). Our tour price included all tips for services. Some of the places were serviced by horse-drawn carriages. On one occasion when we returned from a short journey, the driver asked for 'baksheesh'. When challenged by our guide, he said is was only for his horse. I still regret not having a peppermint in my pocket. The driver obviously did not want to be crossed off the list. The Temple of Philae was most interesting. A visit by 'felucca' – flat-bottomed sailing boat – to the Aga Khan Mausoleum, Kitchener garden and elephantine hands, made it a pleasant day. As dusk fell, we returned to our boat, competing with the other boats, and a sing-song. I think we were the winner, first home anyway. Our boat, the *Nile Rhapsody* was modern, and one of very few that could navigate up the Nile all the way, because the great river is shallow. It was also our fortieth wedding anniversary and a bouquet of red roses for the lady and a bottle of wine with the boat's compliments came as a pleasant surprise. An artistic display and a belly dancer shaking it all about concluded a memorable evening.

South Africa

South Africa has all the ingredients for an ideal holiday destination for the British visitor – spectacular scenery, wildlife and game reserves, golden beaches and sophisticated cities. Add to these the exceptional value for money which the country offers and you have an unbeatable combination. If offers a wonderful opportunity to visit a country which I believe can rival all others – at affordable prices. A discovery of a world in one country. Cape Town, with the sparkling waters of the Atlantic Ocean, and the imposing backdrop of the Table Mountain, is one of the world's most beautiful cities. With winter in the northern hemisphere, the warmth of a southern summer is a striking contrast. You feel at ease amidst a cross-cultural community in this area. We paid a visit to 'Stollenbosh' – one of the earliest white settlements, a famous wine-growing area. It is also where the Huguenots established a headquarters when driven from Europe.

South Africa is vast, beautiful and rich. Only now is it emerging from painful years of internal argument and international condemnation. Only relatively recently has it been reintroduced to international sport.

It was the policy of the South African government to maintain white supremacy through apartheid – I take no sides in that argument but such a policy upset many other countries and created the isolation of South Africa.

In terms of sheer geography South Africa straddles the sea route from the Middle East to Europe and the United States around the Cape of Good Hope, a route taken by oil tankers that are too big for the Suez Canal.

The country has enormous mineral wealth, from gold – it is the biggest producer of gold in the world – diamonds, uranium and silver, to coal and natural gas, asbestos, chrome, copper, iron, magnesium, nickel and platinum.

We went to the Cape of Good Hope, a scenic route through the best holiday area where the rich and the famous live. All along the coastal road is a narrow strip of land, perhaps two miles wide, where there is almost all-year-round sunshine. To the north, the ground rises almost vertical and the top is covered almost all the time in grey mist. The same often applies to Table Mountain when the locals say, 'It has a tablecloth on today.' Our tour included a visit to a crocodile farm. While a crocodile lays about fifty eggs a year, the sex of their offspring is determined by the temperature while incubating. Two degrees will make the difference and all the hatch will be of the same sex. An ostrich farm was also interesting, and we saw three ostrich races. I always thought the meat would be tough, but it was not so. Only the slow production rate makes it expensive. While the hens in South Africa lay approximately sixty-five eggs a year, in Europe this number drops to forty-five. And the mating is only one to one, or one to two at best; until artificial insemination can bring this cost down, ostrich meat will stay expensive.

A visit to a Zulu settlement was quite interesting – traditional dancing to Zulu music. All the girls are topless and come in all sizes – large, medium and small, like anywhere in the world. Every settlement has a chief, a medical man and we have been assured that eighty per cent of them would pass medical examinations in the western world. Another important person is the clairvoyant. If any crime has been committed, which is very rare, all the people are called to the normal meeting place (corral), where the offence is announced and everybody is invited to disclose all they know about it. This process is deliberately very slow. It can take two or three hours. Every member so firmly believes in the infallibility of clairvoyance that after a little while the guilty party will perspire and feel so restless that it is easy to identify s/he; the culprit will leave the compound and go out in the bush, never to be seen alive again. The scavengers will mostly deal with remains in nature's way. If anybody should be found, they have never shown any signs of injury. Whether it is the shame of being rejected by the people or the very strong will to die has never been proven.

The main attraction of the country is, of course, the wildlife. Kruger Park is world-famous. There are African elephants, which are much bigger than the Indian ones, giraffes with their enquiring looks on their faces, and lions. They are truly kings of the jungle. While the female prides are plentiful, the king is more elusive. Much bigger than the female, the face full of deep furrows like a grumpy old monarch with a mane adding to his decoration, he is lazy and does not very often join in the hunting – only when his considerable strength is required for something really big, like a wildebeest or zebra, which graze and travel in large mixed herds. Impalas probably provide most meals. In life, it is normal for the male of the species to look for love-life. But in lion love-life, Leo cannot be bothered. It is initiated by the female, and lasts for about a week. Warthogs can be seen quite often. We were fortunate to see a pack of wild dogs. Life in the parks usually centres around the water holes. All the sightseeing in Kruger Park is done in mini-buses and the animals take no notice of the vehicles.

From the park to Johannesburg, we have seen many large fertile farms with pineapples, hemp, sugar cane, and other crops. We had booked for a three-day extension to see the Victoria Waterfalls. It would have involved a three-day stay in Johannesburg – and our guide advised us against it. He said, 'It is not a very nice place for "foriegners" to be in alone. People look under the bed before turning the lights out.' So we stopped at the airport and came home with the rest. Chaos reigned at the airport. Our guide said, 'It is always like that but not to worry.' Off he went and came back with the foreman and a trolley. His boss ordered him to get another group to the check-in first – but to no avail. Our guide knew the price and paid up – and the foreman knew he had to deliver.

Mediterranean and Black Sea Cruise

A journey through Italy is a scenic idyll. The northern borderland embraces really spectacular Alpine scenery, culminating in Mont Blanc, massive on the French frontier, and the Matterhorn on the Swiss side. There are small glaciers in places and splendid ski slopes have popularised winter resorts.

Many of the valleys are closed in to form lakes. The changeover from the Alps into the great northern plain is abrupt and the prosperity in this area is evident. Going southwards the climate grows perceptibly warmer, the sky bluer, the people more outgoing.

The beauty of such a cruise is that you leave one port in the evening and the next morning you are somewhere completely different. A guided bus tour takes you to the most scenic places around that area and you learn about its history as you go. One of the most interesting tours led us to the cone of Vesuvius. At present it is quiet, but was terrifyingly active in the past, as in AD79 when it destroyed Pompei. All those who watched Frankie Howerd in *Up Pompei* thought it was just put up for the cameras. They would never believe how factual it was: piped water in AD79, bathhouses for the community, the roads with the raised middle for horses, the ovens for bread-baking.

In Italy, you begin to understand that history is not something belonging to a distant past. The plain fact is history is all around you. You almost get the impression that some places have existed since time began. Yet, despite its sense of antiquity, Italy as a political unit is little more than 125 years old.

In 1946, Italy became a Republic and the Christian Democrats have dominated Italian politics ever since. But governments have rarely lasted long; in fact, Italy has had more changes of government than any other European power – and to some of us it may seem that the Italians are frequently on strike.

The living quarters with balconies centred around the main square where the orgies took place. These secret quarters have very faded drawings where you want to cover up the children's eyes. Yes, that is not only where it all happened, but also how it happened. The fact that all was buried under mountains of ashes accounts for it being so well preserved and new discoveries are still being made.

The Benedictine Abbey of Monte Cassino was totally destroyed by the allies during the Second World War. It has since been painstakingly rebuilt. The German forces defended the mountain for six months, but the Italian guide firmly denies that any German soldier ever entered the Benedictine Abbey itself and pointed to the official records kept there. On our way down by bus, two middle-aged English ladies in the seat in front of us said that the Italians should never be allowed to say such things in their official records because that is not what we were told during the war.

Sicily is an enlarged miniature of everything Italian. The class difference is pronounced. The hereditary power of the aristocratic families and the chronic unemployment perpetuate vast differences between the classes. There is no opportunity – or hope – of climbing the ladder. An air of resignation is all around you. On our visit to Taormina, we passed the still active volcano of Etna. Our memories are sparkling blue sea, a mixture of old and new – the 'Haves' and the 'Have-nots'.

After Sicily, we had a full day at sea on our way to Turkey.

Turkey forms the bridge between Europe and Asia, with land on both continents. It guards the only sea passage between the Black Sea and the Mediterranean, which flows through the Bosphorus. Istanbul is full of beauty and mystery; outstanding masterpieces of monumental architecture, like the Blue Mosque and the Ayosofya Mosque. There is also the Grand Bazaar, 3,000 shops selling anything and everything.

The journey through the Bosphorus provided a good comparison between the splendour on the left and industrial Asia Minor on the right.

The Black Sea – Yalta is the tourist health resort on the Crimea, bedecked with flowering shrubs and plants, and has attracted holidaymakers and the ailing since the early nineteenth century. In February 1945, the small resort of Livadiya made history as the setting for the critical Yalta Conference, which planned the final stages of the Second World War and the division of power in post-war Europe. We were shown the room where Stalin and Roosevelt had a secret meeting behind locked doors, where important decisions regarding Germany and its people following the war were made. I don't think the victorious powers are very proud of what happened in 1945/46, especially America. Our next port of call was Odessa, where we were entertained by the ballet *Die Fleidermaus*, and *Romeo and Juliet*.

Then it was back to Turkey again and the ruins of Ephesus, the legendary site of classical marvels.

Highlights of the Mediterranean

Our holiday plans in 1999 were upset by a week in hospital.

My private collection of daffodils I had handed to our grandchildren were due to be lifted, sterilised and re-planted into new ground. We sometimes feel we are indispensable and this was one such occasion. The collection consists of approximately 350 crosses and every one had to be kept separate, replanted and marked for selection over the next few years. Although no longer mine, I still enjoy being involved. All safely planted back, we were ready for our holiday in September: a cruise to see the highlights of the Mediterranean aboard the *Albatross 99*.

On day one, we sailed overnight to St Malo in France for a day's sightseeing. St Malo is a wonderful example of a walled town, and the view from the ramparts is spectacular. It is also the gateway to the magnificent beaches of Brittany and Mont St Michel, the medieval cathedral city built on an island.

We left at eight-ten p.m. heading in the direction of Vigo in Spain, spending the next day at sea exploring the boat and entertainment offered.

In the evening was the captain's welcoming cocktail party, when all the ladies dressed in their finery and most men in their evening suits. All drinks were free on this cruise and served with a smile wherever you were. Connie and I indulged only in the wine with lunch and dinner and one at the evening entertainments.

The following night we entered the Bay of Biscay and a rising wind. By midnight, a full-blown gale was rocking the boat, which was fully stabilised and, with our cabin in the middle of the boat we were in the best place. It was like being rocked to sleep.

After some time I woke to a very gentle stroking over the duvet, starting from the feet upwards as far as the knees and eventually returning to the feet again very softly, almost soothing. This was repeated several times. Earlier I had heard that there was a curse on the *Albatross* because a sailor had shot one long ago and the bird was now almost extinct. I do not believe in ghosts but was I to be proved wrong? The curiosity was almost killing me. If it was the ghost of the *Albatross* then I was enjoying its company. I have never heard of anybody being killed by a ghost. It must have been the best part of an hour when I folded the duvet back against the cupboards at the sidewall and sat on the side of the bed with my feet on the floor. There was sufficient light in the cabin to see, and, feeling over the duvet, the funny sensation had stopped. Like many good ghost stories, there was a logical explanation. Beside the bed were two wall cupboards, about two foot six long and fifteen inches high, hinged at the far end. Every time the boat swayed, the doors swung to and fro, gently, brushing over the duvet. As the boat swayed the other way, so did the door. When I folded the duvet back the movement stopped because it was high enough to stop the door from swinging. So I still don't believe in ghosts!

Then I went to the porthole and watched the sea in brilliant moonlight. It looked very angry with the spray coming past our porthole. I went back to bed and fell asleep almost at once.

Breakfast was always an open sitting and served to order or in the cabins. The ladies, looking so elegant the evening before, wriggling past the ship's captain, were now moving across the dining room floor looking very different – more like the ship's cat crossing the deck in a gale.

Vigo, sitting at the head of the longest of the Catalonian fjords, provided good protection against the rough sea and the sea was normal again. The captain said that he had been travelling this route for six years and it was the roughest he had ever experienced. Its setting is spectacular. It is also the starting place for the memorial excursion to Santiago de Compastella, the final resting place of St John and which, next to Rome and Jerusalem, is the third most important pilgrimage site in Christendom.

Then it was on to Lisbon, sitting proudly on the River Tagus, it is one of the most beautiful capitals in Europe. Lisbon is another world away from the oxcarts creaking their way up rough hillside tracks. The country's industry focuses mainly in the districts of Lisbon and Setubal. Nearby is Simba, described by Lord Byron as his Eden. Lisbon bristles with museums, galleries, shops and stores, parks and gardens.

Next came Gibraltar. Rising out of the sea off the coast of southern Spain, the Rock remains staunchly British. Here you find familiar red telephone boxes, bobbies on the beat and wonderful tax-free shopping. A trip to the top of the rock by cable car is rewarded with magnificent views and no visit to Gibraltar is complete without seeing the colony of Barbary Apes, whose presence, according to Winston Churchill, assures that the rock will remain British.

The next destination was Palma, Majorca, and it provided us with a new experience in our life. In the evenings, there was normally a short talk about the next port of call and excursions available. We were warned to be aware of pick-pockets in Palma; they usually worked in groups of three. One would push you down from behind, the other two would then hold you down and within seconds watches, valuables and money would all be gone. They did not warn us about old ladies looking like poor peasants, trying to sell you buttonholes, and working in twos!

Connie and I went to town in the tour bus with a group of others, getting off at the beginning of the town, admiring a waterfall display and pleasant gardens. Whilst strolling towards the town we saw a horse tied to a lamp-post, with a carriage and a notice offering rides through the town and the price. The driver was nowhere to be seen and we decided to leave the ride until later. We counted out the money required and set it aside in the top pocket of my shirt. We had not moved more than a few feet when two old ladies stood in front of us and pinned a rose on Connie's lapel and the other said, 'A carnation for the gentleman,' pushing a very wilted one in the top of my shirt pocket, saying, 'Only two pence.' As I turned towards Connie I could see the other woman pulling the rose from Connie's jacket, and both of them moving across the street with remarkable speed. We did not even realise we had been robbed. When I went into a newsagent to buy an English newspaper I searched through my pockets. We instantly looked at each other and Connie said, 'Well, I'll be… .' We both instantly knew what had happened. Well, Palma is a city of majestic monuments, super shops and a host of attractions – but a bad memory for us. The loss of about £6 is a small price for a valuable lesson.

At Minorca we met beautiful scenery and soft, sandy beaches. Port Mahon lies at the eastern end of the island on a cliff-fringed table of rock making an inlet about three miles long. Its sheltered position makes it one of the best natural harbours of the Mediterranean.

Our next destination was one of the lesser-known holiday destinations, but one of the most interesting. Ajaccie, in Corsica. Christened the 'Island of Light' and an island of beauty, Corsica offers a great variety of scenery, from the mountains of the interior to the rocky bays and sandy beaches of the glorious coastline. The luxuriant growth of vegetation, forests, vineyards and an abundance of flowers inspired its most famous son, Napoleon, to say that he could recognise Corsica with his eyes closed from its perfume alone.

After Corsica we moved on to Genoa, known as 'Genoa the Proud'. The seafaring traditions here go back centuries. Genoa's majestic buildings are set in a great semi-circle around the port and the lower city begins immediately behind the docks. The historic quarter is a maze of traffic-free alleys, flanked by palaces seven or eight stories high that keeps the little lanes in perpetual shadow. Along the Via Venti Settembre you will discover fantastically decorated palaces in the *art nouveau* style. Via Dante leads to picturesque Porte Soprano, with its medieval towers and adjacent garden. Here you will find a small medieval house that is reputed to be the birthplace of Christopher Columbus. An excursion to the small town of Porta Fina is an experience in itself: a memory to be treasured. In Genoa approximately half of the passengers disembarked and were replaced by others for the second cruise.

Then it was on to Barcelona in Spain, site of the 1992 Olympic Games, and the birthplace of the innovative architect, Gaudi. Much of his work is breathtaking. Strolling along the ramparts, browsing in the shop and boutiques, sitting at the pavement cafe we were in awe of his magnificent cathedral. The next day was a day at sea, a day of rest.

On our way to Tunisia, an interesting speaker, amongst others, told us his experience as ambassador around the world: fascinating stuff, enjoying the good life, free drinks and tasting the exquisite specialities from the kitchen. Tunis gave us the taste of Africa with a French accent.

The Tunisian capital is a city of broad, tree-lined avenues and mysterious labyrinthine covered markets. It was the starting point for excursions to Carthage and Kairouan, the main Islamic city in North Africa, and the fourth 'Saint' city in the Islamic world. The markets are an experience to be savoured: a multitude of anything and everything.

Bargaining is essential. If you pay the asking price you are either an American or mad, or both. Many of the articles you can purchase for as little as one-seventh of the asking price.

Labour-consuming products can be good buys because of the very low labour costs.

Next was another island: Malta, the George Cross island of Malta. The Venetian fort still guards the port of Valetta. From the upper Barracca Gardens you can enjoy a panoramic view of the natural harbours and historic cities of Senglea, Cospicua and Vittorios. Malta is famous too for its exquisite Medina glass, not to mention the sun-drenched climate.

Now we came to secretive Sicily, the largest of all Mediterranean islands. Its most notable landmark is the massive snow-covered cone of Mount Etna, Europe's largest active volcano. It has magnificent scenery, beautiful beaches and a great range of ancient remains, including the best preserved Greek Temples in the world. We brought back an elephant carved out of Mount Etna's lava in memory of this beautiful place. Our guide pointed out two hills in the distance – a larger version of our 'uneven road' sign. This is known locally as the 'Breast of Sophia Loren' – when she was younger!

We ended at Naples. It stands in the shadow of Mount Vesuvius and is the gateway to the ruins of the ancient city of Pompeii, which was engulfed in volcanic dust and thus preserved for all time in the first century AD. Just along the coast is Sorrento with splendid panoramic views over Capri and the Gulfs of Marina Grande and Marina Piccola. From there, back to Genoa, disembarking and home. A remarkable and enjoyable holiday all round: a good ship, excellent cabins, fine food, good company and free wine.

It was nice to be home again, the green fields of southern England, cows grazing in them. There is no place like home.

Rudi and Connie

*T*ogether,
we've worked hard
to get where we are today.
Together,
we've raised a wonderful family
that has brought our lives
much richness and joy …
Together,
we've supported each other
through ups and downs,
through the good times
and through life's challenges.
Together,
we've grown in so many ways …

I have one last wish. At the end of my days, may my ashes be scattered in a corner where daffodils grow, so in the following spring when they come up to flower, I will be amongst friends again.

END